THE
ANNA
ANOINTING

MICHELLE McCLAIN-WALTERS

CHARISMA
HOUSE

Most CHARISMA HOUSE BOOK GROUP products are available at special quantity discounts for bulk purchase for sales promotions, premiums, fund-raising, and educational needs. For details, write Charisma House Book Group, 600 Rinehart Road, Lake Mary, Florida 32746, or telephone (407) 333-0600.

THE ANNA ANOINTING by Michelle McClain-Walters
Published by Charisma House
Charisma Media/Charisma House Book Group
600 Rinehart Road
Lake Mary, Florida 32746
www.charismahouse.com

Parts of this book were taken from *The Prophetic Advantage* and *The Deborah Anointing*.

Copyright © 2017 by Michelle McClain-Walters
All rights reserved

Cover design by Lisa Rae McClure
Design Director: Justin Evans

Visit the author's website at www.michellemcclainwalters.com.

Library of Congress Cataloging-in-Publication Data:
Names: McClain-Walters, Michelle, author.
Title: The Anna anointing / Michelle McClain-Walters.
Description: Lake Mary, Florida : Charisma House, 2017. | Includes bibliographical references and index.
Identifiers: LCCN 2017003793| ISBN 9781629989471 (trade paper : alk. paper) |
    ISBN 9781629989488 (ebook : alk. paper)
Subjects: LCSH: Anna (Biblical prophetess) | Christian women--Religious life.
Classification: LCC BS2452.A5 M33 2017 | DDC 226/.092--dc23
LC record available at https://lccn.loc.gov/2017003793

17 18 19 20 21 — 9 8 7 6 5 4 3 2
Printed in the United States of America

CONTENTS

Introduction

> I sought for a man among them who would build up the
> hedge and stand in the gap before Me for the land so that I
> would not destroy it, but I found no one.
>
> —EZEKIEL 22:30

GOD IS IN pursuit of you. The heart of God is searching for those who would answer the call to stand in the gap. The gap is the breach between God and our society. Satan has blinded the hearts of many. Our generation has become highly humanistic. Many want power without God. Many come to the church for an experience rather than a relationship with the true and living God.

If someone doesn't occupy the gap, destruction can occur. Someone must stand in the gap between God and man to cry for mercy and grace for this generation. God is seeking women who will take up the mantle of prayer to release healing, deliverance, and glory upon the earth.

The noteworthy life of Anna the prophetess is a prophetic picture of standing in the gap that is of benefit to the church today. In one of the darkest times of human history, when Israel was waiting on the promised Messiah, a time of great transition and pain, God raised up Anna. God is releasing the spirit of grace and supplication upon women to sustain long seasons of prayer and fasting. They will pray and proclaim the revelation of Jesus to a lost and dying generation.

Become a Woman Who Moves the Hand of God

This book will focus on the power of a consecrated life. It will focus on what happens when a woman dedicates her life in service to the Lord. Anna did not have *political* influence—she had *spiritual* influence. Anna was a woman of persistence, hope, and power. Her prayers and fasts were instrumental in birthing the first coming of Christ. God is mustering an army of women with the Anna anointing who will cry out until the knowledge of the glory of the Lord covers the earth as the waters cover the sea (Isa. 13:1–5; Hab. 2:14). Those with the Anna anointing will be set as watchmen in the temple, giving the Lord no rest until revival breaks out in the land. They will labor in intercession for the release of God's power to win the lost, revive the church, and impact society with the gospel of the kingdom. These women will touch the heart of God as they cry out with heartfelt prayers for the sins of this nation. They will be equipped with fire, zeal, and power to proclaim the name of Jesus Christ to those who look for redemption. God is awakening a prayer movement that will release the power of His kingdom. Through the power of prayer we will see righteousness, peace, and joy in the Holy Ghost on the earth once again. The modern-day Anna will pray effective, fervent prayers that will make tremendous power available to this generation (James 5:16).

We have reached a critical point in our nation's history. We need people who will once again contend for the faith. *Contend* means "to fight for something while striving against the difficulties that hinder its release."[1] The modern-day Anna will have a burden to see this generation walk in everything that God has purposed. Her main objective is to pray for the advancement of the kingdom of God. She makes a lamentation concerning our powerlessness and spiritual barrenness.

This is a time of transition into the fullness of new covenant power. Jesus represents a transition from the old covenant to the new covenant. A modern-day Anna will fast and pray to see the fullness of the new covenant implemented upon the earth.

The new covenant is more glorious than the old covenant. People under the new covenant experience God's glory, miracles, healing, prophetic ministry, and much more. The glory of the new covenant is the transforming power of the indwelling Holy Spirit. As part of the new covenant, God promises to write His Word on our hearts (Jer. 31:33).

In His sovereign power the Lord stirs nations and people to be His agents on the earth. I believe that an army of praying, prophesying, and preaching women will be His weapons of indignation. *Indignation* is defined as "strong displeasure at something considered unjust, offensive, insulting, or base; righteous anger."[2]

When the Lord wants a task completed and His purposes fulfilled, He will awaken a person or people to accomplish His will on the earth. The Lord is mustering an army to cry out in prayer and intercession against the wicked schemes of the enemy in the land. This army will serve God in fasting and prayer, as did Anna the prophetess until revival and glory fill the earth.

> The LORD has opened His armory and has brought out
> the weapons of His indignation, for this is the work of
> the Lord GOD of hosts.
>
> —JEREMIAH 50:25

God is calling us to be history makers. God wants to turn the disaster zone into a revival center. He wants to release the blessing of the Holy Spirit through our prayers. He wants to release power. Where the people of God gather, He wants to develop pockets of mercy, cities of refuge. He will release power and supernatural protection, provision, and direction in different places. The reason He holds back until His people respond is because He wants His people to be the agent of change before the throne of grace. He wants people in intimacy with Him and in partnership with Him to be the vehicle through which He releases blessing to the world.

In a world of people searching for significance, looking for a place to belong, wandering aimlessly about, and desperately seeking security, God is awakening in individuals a deep desire to know His divine calling and destiny for their lives. Some are called to be lawyers or doctors, and some are called to serve the Lord with fasting and prayer in the house of the Lord.

As this awakening in the human heart is filling the land, the enemy is simultaneously releasing identity confusion and rebellion against God in the hearts of the same human beings. The spirit of Babylon is blinding the hearts and minds of individuals to the truth that Jesus Christ is the only way to salvation. The spirit of Babylon represents the power of darkness that seeks to enslave and oppress mankind. This demonic spirit assignment is to erase identities and the true purpose of God from the conscience of human beings. It is a spirit that influences man to build a society in defiance to God similar to the Tower of Babel in Scripture. The spirit of Babylon promotes a system that is in complete rebellion to and enmity against the standards of God. This demonic spirit's modus operandi infuses confusion into human hearts. It is what I call "gross darkness."

God in His wisdom is mustering up an army of His sanctified ones, those called to a special purpose: lifting up their voices to heaven and wailing, releasing the day of the Lord. This army will be sharp threshing instruments in the hand of God (Isa. 41:15). They will have an understanding of the Spirit of God and make room for His hand to move upon the earth. God will use women in prayer to radically change the course and history of nations.

Become Armed and Ready

This radical call to women to be influential and powerful will require training and equipping. It will involve sacrifice and faith to believe God in the face of adversity and opposition. The greatest teachers will be life and your experience with the Lord. God calls us to embrace His future with such a passion that even the present can be given up for that promised future. God calls us to trust the Promise Giver, who is a promise keeper, with all our heart, soul, mind, and strength.

Many of you have faced adversity as did our heroine Anna, but through prayer and perseverance you will learn to use that adversity for your advantage. God is raising up an army of women who will be anchored in hope and determined to dream again and leave a lasting legacy on the earth. He is empowering women with the spirit of prayer and intercession to bring healing and deliverance to the nations of the earth. The Lord is causing women to awaken to their inner strength and arise to their full potential. God is calling an army of warrior women to abide in Him, begin to view the world from His perspective, and recognize how He is calling each one to be involved in the great battle for the harvest of souls. This battle will be fought and won by kneeling on the promises of God for our land.

As the Lord begins to direct you to embrace your calling and the stirring in your heart for His destiny and purpose for you, I believe that you will begin to take on a similar divine urgency and sense of responsibility for things greater than yourself. I believe that you will begin to see yourself as a woman of influence, conviction, and power. A divinely inspired cry will come out of your spirit: "Lord, come and heal our land!"

The passion and righteous indignation of the Lord is arising in the hearts of women to take up the sword of the Spirit in prayer, to touch heaven through prayer and intercession, and to bring reformation on the earth. God is going to begin to quicken your spirit with an anointing to influence leaders in various spheres and redeem them for the kingdom of God. This influence will occur through the power of prayer.

I believe that God will inspire you with a prophetic anointing to speak the right words, to awaken an army of men and women in powerful places, and to advocate and endorse kingdom rule and advancement. I see you taking on the mantle of Anna and walking in the anointing of prayer and revelation to bring solutions. You will take on the characteristics of the anointing and see amazing things happen in your life and the lives of those you love.

Sound the Alarm

The purpose of this book is to sound the alarm and remove the scales of discouragement and defeat that have numbed women to the pain and devastation around them. The Holy Spirit is leading and challenging women to discover their passion and purpose by rising up and taking hold of the power God has given them, and by waking up and changing their sphere of influence in the world. New assignments and prophetic marching orders are being activated and given to women to penetrate the world with the gospel of the kingdom.

God is raising up a generation of women who will operate in the fullness of His glory and power. Joel 2:28–30 speaks of a day when the Lord will pour out His Spirit on the sons and daughters, and as a result they *all* will prophesy. The pouring out of God's Spirit is the ability not only to prophesy but also to pray effectively, love deeply, and lead fearlessly. Truly an army is being raised up, and Jesus is calling all of His troops to be adequately trained and equipped to pray effective, fervent prayers. The Lord is teaching our hands to war and our fingers to fight (Ps. 144:1).

In times of uncertainty and turbulence the Lord has given me a mandate to raise up a company of women who have confidence in His sovereignty, a compass of righteousness in their hearts, and the Word of the Lord in their mouths. It is my passion to encourage women to take their place in the kingdom and fulfill the mandate and mission to go into the entire world preaching the gospel and making disciples of the nations.

What Is the Anna Anointing?

> And there was Anna a prophetess, a daughter of Phanuel, of the tribe of Asher. She was of a great age and had lived with her husband seven years from her virginity. And she was a widow of about eighty-four years of age who did not depart from the temple, but served God with fasting and prayer night and day. Coming at that moment she gave thanks to the Lord and spoke of Him to all those who looked for the redemption of Jerusalem.
> —LUKE 2:36–38

The clearest description of the Anna anointing is found in Luke 2:36–38. Notice she is called a prophetess, one who served the Lord day and night in fasting and prayer. She was empowered by the spirit of prophecy to testify of Jesus to those who looked for redemption. Anna was a woman in whom the offices of the prophet, the intercessor, and the evangelist converged. God is empowering women with the same grace in this generation. Not every woman with an Anna anointing will be a prophet, but she will have a prophetic spirit. The Anna anointing is an expression of the prophetic anointing, through night-and-day fasting and prayer and the spirit of prophecy to testify of Jesus through prophetic evangelism. Scripture does not state that Anna actually gave a prophetic word, but her actions were prophetic.

The life of Anna the prophetess is a prophetic picture for

women today. God is in pursuit of a generation of women who will fulfill His mandate of protecting the earth from destruction and petitioning His heart for the release of glory upon the earth. God is using unlikely candidates. He is using women who may have felt left out by society, who have overcome great adversity and trauma. He is using overcomers. Anna was widowed at a young age, but she overcame great loss and found hope for her future in the presence of the Lord. Anna fasted and prayed in the temple night and day for over sixty years just before the first coming of Jesus. Anna was the first evangelist in the New Testament. She proclaimed the truth of God to all of those who looked for redemption.

The Holy Spirit is raising up women akin to Anna to pray effectively, fast consistently, and preach prophetically. The Holy Spirit is raising up women who will operate with the spirit of prophecy to testify of Jesus with signs and wonders following them. These women will be the expression of Revelation 22:17: "And the Spirit and the bride say, 'Come!' And let him who hears say, 'Come!' And let him who thirsts come" (NKJV). The heart of the modern-day Anna will be synchronized with the Holy Spirit. They will have a grace to pray the promises of God accurately on the earth. They will give a prophetic invitation for the Lord to come. I am not talking about coming as in the Rapture, but instead coming to reveal His love and empower His church; I am talking about coming revival and glory. The Anna anointing is stirred up as women begin to live as intercessors, working for the fulfillment of the Great Commission, the spreading of the gospel to all nations.

Four Keys to Activate the Anna Anointing

There are four keys to activate the Anna anointing:

1. Prayer—The primary anointing of Anna was to develop a listening heart that prayed fervent, effective

prayers according to the heart and mind of the Lord. She cried out to the Lord for justice and righteousness to fill the earth.

2. Worship—Ministering in the temple is worshipping God. Anna developed a lifestyle of worship. She presented her body as a living sacrifice to God. Her power to recognize the Messiah came from her lifestyle of worship. Anna demonstrated the revelation of the power of a woman of worship. Worship is the primary key to unlock the supernatural resources of heaven.

3. Perseverance—Serving for sixty years before seeing the promise, Anna developed tenacity and perseverance. Anna learned how to set her affections on things above. As women, many times we can be weighed down with the cares of this world, but those with an Anna anointing will understand the power of a focused life.

4. Watchfulness—Anna was a watchman/prophetess. She set up a vigil around the promises of God. *Vigil* can be defined as "a period of staying awake to…call public attention to something."[3] I believe there is significance to praying day and night. Anna developed a prayer watch around seeing the promises of God fulfilled, and the modern-day Anna will do the same. The modern-day Anna will spend her time watching and praying for the promises of God to be fulfilled on the earth. She will fulfill Isaiah 62:6: "I have set watchmen on your walls, O Jerusalem, who shall never hold their peace day nor night. You who remind the Lord, do not keep silent." The modern-day Anna will develop a relentless, urgent, watching anointing.

The modern-day Anna will live a life of holy abandonment to the purposes of the Lord Jesus. God in His sovereignty is creating spiritual unrest in the hearts of women, causing a great cry to arise for justice and peace. We are tired of seeing our children die in the streets and violent and angry men terrorizing our nation. It is time for the women with the Anna anointing to arise.

Three Hindrances to the Anna Anointing

In a world where women are always challenged to become more and engage in more activities, the calling of Anna could be looked upon as a waste of time. Our society defines success based on what we do and how much stuff we accumulate. The Anna calling is solely based on obedience to the Lord. If you are going to embrace the Anna anointing, you must free yourself from the opinions of men. The modern-day Anna must choose to live a life of abandonment to the purposes of the Lord. We must wholeheartedly live a life of sowing to the Spirit. Women with the Anna anointing will live lives of sacrifice, understanding that in this world and the world to come we will reap a harvest of great rewards. Anna did not focus on herself. She focused on the kingdom of God and spreading the goodness of the Messiah. She did not allow any hindrances to stand in her way. These are some of the things that can hinder being able to fully function in an Anna anointing:

1. Fear of man—An "it doesn't take all of that" mentality can get in the way of our anointing to serve as Anna did. Proverbs 29:25 states that the fear of man brings a snare, but those who trust in God are safe. The calling of Anna requires a conscious decision to live a life of holiness and consecration. This choice is contrary to the self-centered lifestyle of many in our

culture. Women with the calling of Anna cannot concern themselves with what others think about their decisions. The lifestyle of the modern-day Anna will be akin to a slap in the face to apathetic Christianity.

2. False burdens and a works mentality—We are to labor in prayer for the kingdom to increase. The error of the church of Ephesus was to do kingdom work without prayer and intimacy with Jesus (Rev. 2:4). Those with an Anna anointing must be careful to not bear false burdens or develop a works mentality. The Lord wants us to come and learn from Him, for His yoke is easy and His burden is light (Matt. 11:28–30). The Lord gives more if we ask for more, and in the process of speaking to God and bringing Him these requests, we develop our relationship with Him, and that is what He really wants.

3. Isolation mentality—Anna was a perfect example for the modern-day intercessor. She was balanced in her service to the Lord. She not only spent hours in the presence of the Lord, but she also ministered to the lost. It has been my experience that some intercessors prefer to stay insulated in the presence of the Lord and never interact with the world. This intercessor will pray to the Lord of the harvest to send forth laborers, never realizing that he or she is one of the laborers.

How to Overcome Hindrances
to the Anna Anointing

Even though Anna was a widow, she didn't pray as a widow. She understood that she was a bride. As the bride of Christ we are yoked to the purposes of Jesus, our Bridegroom. Our desire to please Him outweighs the fear of man. When we relate to Jesus as our Bridegroom, understanding His affection for us, we are made perfect in love. The Bible tells that perfect love casts out fear (1 John 4:18). Receiving God's love releases boldness and courage to fulfill your assignment in the earth.

There is no one closer to a bridegroom than his bride. Intimacy and partnership are the motivation of a bride, not dead works. Serving the Lord from the perspective of a bride delivers us from tradition and from ministry burnout. As a bride we learn to lean and depend on the grace of God to do the works of ministry. Your mentality shifts from working for Him to working with Him. As a bride you will learn to cast your cares and burdens upon the Lord because of covenantal love.

The mystery of marriage is that two people become one. When we as Christians live from the bridal paradigm, we learn to embrace Jesus's affection for mankind and for us, which empowers us to serve Him. Jesus asked Peter, "Do you love Me?," and then said, "Feed My sheep." One of the expressions and demonstrations of loving God is loving people. The bridal paradigm breaks isolation and empowers you not only to pray for the sheep but also to feed them with knowledge and wisdom. His desires become your desires. We partner with Him to do the work of the kingdom.

If you're going to be effective in life, your identity must be rooted in the covenantal love of Christ. Your life situation and social status do not define who you are before the throne of God. You may be single, divorced, or widowed, but in the eyes of God you're the bride of Christ. You can access all the privileges of a bride. I challenge you to search the Scriptures and meditate on the times God refers to Himself as your husband. This will bring great peace and assurance of the protection, provision, and providential care of the Lord. Meditating on the nature of God as a husband will empower you to go to the throne of grace in prayer to obtain mercy and find grace to help in every situation.

> For your Maker is your husband, the LORD of Hosts is His name; and your Redeemer is the Holy One of Israel; He shall be called the God of the whole earth. For the LORD has called you.
>
> —ISAIAH 54:5–6

Prayers to Activate the Anna Anointing

> God anointed Jesus of Nazareth with the Holy Spirit and with power, who went about doing good and healing all who were oppressed by the devil, for God was with Him.
>
> —ACTS 10:38

Anoint means "to smear or rub with oil or perfume for religious purposes." [4] As you pray for the Anna anointing, God will anoint you and set you apart for divine use. In this time of consecration and separation to the work of the Lord, you must be delivered from the opinions of men. The anointing makes you responsible and accountable to the person who does the anointing. When you are anointed, you are empowered by God to accomplish a task. An anointing provides safety and protection—no one is allowed to touch you, not even demons and devils.

The Anna anointing will empower you to touch the heart of God in heaven to bring change upon the earth. Here are three prayers you can pray to begin to activate this powerful anointing in your life.

Father, I cry out to You for an impartation of the spirit of grace and supplication. I believe that the effective prayers of the righteous make Your heavenly power available upon the earth. I lay aside my dreams and plans and press in to Your agenda and Your assignment for my life. I know that Your plans for me are good and not evil. Your plans for the earth are good and not evil. Lord, anoint me to partner with You in fulfilling the Great Commission. I find the hope of my future in Your presence. Let the power of the Holy Spirit fill every area of my life with Your wisdom and courage. Amen.

Lord, I pray that You will make me a house of prayer. I believe the core identity of the church is to be a house of prayer for all nations. Lord, my heart's cry is, "Make me a house of prayer." Holy Spirit, fill me with the knowledge of Your will in wisdom and spiritual understanding. Lord, let me be a vessel used for Your glory. Give me the grace to labor in intercession for the release of Your power to win the lost, revive the church, and impact society with the gospel. I yield to the Holy Spirit as He helps my infirmities and teaches me to pray. Give me a steadfast, focused spirit like Anna. I desire to offer my life as a drink offering to You. Let all the days of my life serve Your purposes. Amen.

Father, I choose to be a victor rather than a victim of the circumstances around me. Help me to understand that I am a bride. Release Your power and glory upon my life. I am Your weapon of indignation. I will raise my voice to heaven until I see revival upon the earth. I will not be moved, shaken, or afraid of the gross darkness upon the earth. Let the light of Your glory fill the earth. Whatever adversity I may face, I choose to overcome by the power of Your love. Amen.

Chapter 1

LIFE AFTER LOSS

And there was Anna a prophetess, a daughter of Phanuel, of
the tribe of Asher. She was of a great age and had lived with
her husband seven years from her virginity. And she was a
widow of about eighty-four years of age who did not depart
from the temple, but served God with fasting and prayer
night and day.

—LUKE 2:36–37

ANNA WAS A prophetess, the daughter of Phanuel, of the tribe
of Asher. The significance of Anna's lineage plays a key role in
the power of her story. The women from the tribe of Asher were
apparently so beautiful that men from all the tribes of Israel
wanted to marry them. Men of the highest stature, such as the
high priests, sought their wives among the daughters of Asher.[1]

Asher's daughters were also known as being "lovely and refined,
which made them most appealing to the family of priests. These
women would best understand and support the priest's work,
since they mirrored the core nature of his responsibilities."[2] One
commentary states that the priest "looked for a wife who would
understand the nature of his work, and he found the best candidates amongst the daughters of Asher. Their exquisite modesty
demonstrated an internal commitment to spirit over flesh."[3]

Anna was raised in the Jewish tradition and was taught about
the one true God. Anna was groomed her entire life to love the
things of the spirit over the things of the flesh. She probably got

married around the age of thirteen, when most Jewish girls of that time period got married. I can just picture her as a thirteen-year-old young woman on her wedding day, standing at the altar, full of hopes and dreams about the future. Although there is not anything written about the vocation of her husband, we can speculate that he was a man of great stature. So Anna and her husband ride off into the sunset and live in marital bliss for seven years.

Then came that dreaded moment that changed everything: Anna's husband died. In an instant she went from being a wife to being a widow. Her dreams of being a mother were suddenly taken away by one unforeseeable event.

Much of what we know about Anna is by implication and not direct knowledge. I can only imagine the questions, the grief, and the fear that flooded her heart and mind: "Why me, Lord? Why this? I did everything right! What now? How am I going to survive this?"

What do you do when life throws you a tragic curveball? How do you pick up the shattered pieces of your life when the one thing you've prepared for and dreamed about suddenly slips through your fingers as wind-driven sand? How do you recover when your vision is clouded by pain and your life plunges into despondency and despair? What do you do when a lifelong dream is suddenly taken away from you without warning and through no fault of your own?

As women we all have faced some type of crisis, whether it's a failed marriage, children on drugs, breast cancer or other illness, loss of a job, wrong choices, or as in Anna's case, the sudden death of a husband. *Crisis* can be defined as "a stage in a sequence of events at which the trend of all future events, especially for better or for worse, is determined; turning point; a dramatic emotional or circumstantial upheaval in a person's life" that leads to a "decisive change."[4] The way to overcome every unforeseen crisis is found in the One who is the overcomer: Jesus. Jesus tells us in John 16:33, "In the world you will have tribulation. But be of good cheer. I have overcome the world." This scripture speaks to the providential care of the Lord. *Providence* comes from two Latin words: *pro*, which means "before," and *video*, which means "to see."[5] You can have confidence in Jesus's ability to see what is ahead in your life and arrange provision and power to overcome.

How do you access this overcoming power? My one answer is hope. I'm not referring to wishful thinking. I believe hope is a person, and His name is Jesus. Jesus is hope. He provides hope. Hope is an expectation and confidence to see God's goodness in life's difficult situations. Hope is the anchor of your soul when life is hard to navigate.

When the storms and tribulations of life come crashing in upon you, you can be anchored in Christ and His promise to cause all things to work together for your good. Romans 8:28 says, "We know that all things work together for good to those who love God, to those who are called according to His purpose." The word *know* means "to see; to perceive, notice, discern, discover; understand."[6] I believe Anna's perception and understanding, based on her personal experience with God, prepared her to walk through this hardship. She had already discovered that God was working things together for her good.

God has promised to release His power and wisdom to overcome difficult and seemingly hopeless seasons in your life. Taking hold of this promise from God creates confidence and perseverance instead of anxiety and fear of the future. When you have a purpose and destiny in God, you can be assured that God will cause trauma, tragedies, and disappointments to work together for your good. I am not saying that God causes these traumatic things to happen, but He will use them to get the best out of your life.

God is very intentional about your growth. The correct response to crisis produces perseverance, character, and hope! You must know that surely there is a hope and your future will not be cut off! You will survive.

Finding Hope in the Face of God

Anna allowed the one true God to turn her crisis into an opportunity for growth and grace. Scripture states that she was the daughter of Phanuel. Jewish parents believed that the name of a child was instrumental in forming his or her identity. They believed that the nature, character, and destiny of children should be proclaimed in their names. *Anna* means "grace"[7] and her father's name, *Phanuel*, means "vision of God" or "face of God."[8] Prophetically speaking, a modern-day Anna will seek the face of God in prayer, finding grace to overcome personal and global crises. Anna demonstrated the power of biblical hope. Biblical hope looks away from man to the promises of God. She postured her life in prayer, looking confidently with expectation for great things from God.

If you fast-forward sixty-plus years after Anna's crisis, you find her living in the temple and serving God with fasting and prayer. She was the first woman in the New Testament to be called a prophetess and to proclaim the name of the Lord to all those who were looking for redemption. She redefined what it meant to be a widow. Instead of waiting for someone to have sympathy for her, she used her life to show compassion for the brokenhearted and those dealing with loss. Anna did the work of an evangelist.

You can see from Anna's life how the grace of God took her on a journey to literally see the face of God. What an honor it was to witness the Messiah coming to the temple. If you allow it, God will awaken destiny and purpose in your life and reveal opportunities to do extraordinary things for Him. As a woman with the Anna anointing, two things must be certain in your heart: God is never in crisis, and He is able to turn the misfortunes of your life into miracles. He is able to do exceedingly and abundantly in your life.

Unlikely Allies: Tribulation, Perseverance, Character, and Hope

> We also glory in tribulations, knowing that tribulation produces perseverance; and perseverance, character; and character, hope. Now hope does not disappoint, because the love of God has been poured out in our hearts by the Holy Spirit.
>
> —Romans 5:3–5, nkjv

The ability to have faith in the goodness of God after you go through testing and trials doesn't happen overnight. I want to make it clear that there is a process. It really takes the supernatural help of the Holy Spirit to cultivate perseverance, character, and hope in the midst of crisis. God in His infinite wisdom allows these unlikely allies to connect in the war over the development of your soul. Healing and restoration are not an automatic result of trials. They occur as you respond rightly to God.

During these times the devil wants to fill your heart with sorrow, fear, and, in some cases, anger with God. However, it is the purpose of your Romans 5 allies to give you the capacity to walk in maturity. Often the Lord will not let you solve all of your problems because He wants you to rely on Him. Many times trials and testing will drive you straight into the presence of the Lord.

The devil will use trials to accuse God. The devil tells you that your trials are proof that God doesn't love you, you are a failure who is forgotten by God and destined to fail, and/or Christianity is not real. But you can be confident that God is working even when you cannot see or feel His work.

Anna's life is a perfect example of how trials are meant to lead us to realign our hearts, to resolve to live closer to the Lord, and to press in for the Spirit's breakthrough solution to our problems. Anna was widowed as a young woman in her twenties. She did not run from God but rather dedicated her life in service to Him. I believe cultivation of the three virtues of perseverance, character, and hope allowed Anna to be a consistent, steadfast intercessor who prayed relentless prayers that birthed Christ, the hope of glory, into the earth.

The right response to tragedy produces patience and perseverance, perseverance produces character, and character produces hope. In Romans 12:12 Paul admonishes us to rejoice in hope, be patient or endure trials, and continue steadfast in prayer. The word *endure* in this verse comes from the Greek word *hupomeno*, which means "to hold one's ground in conflict, bear up against adversity, hold out under stress, stand firm, persevere under pressure, wait calmly and courageously. It is not passive resignation to fate and mere patience, but the active, energetic resistance to defeat that allows calm and brave endurance."[9]

Perseverance has its roots in confidence in God. It can be defined as "continued effort to do or achieve something despite difficulties, failure, or opposition."[10] Perseverance is that small voice inside of you that says, "In the midst of my failure I will try again tomorrow." Perseverance lets you keep one foot in front of the other, one day at a time, one moment at a time.

Anna sets a remarkable example of perseverance. It appears that she never became bitter in the midst of her trial. She never lost hope in the promises of God. She believed that she would see the goodness of the Lord—not only for her life but also for the lives of others—for many years.

The time frame between Anna's loss and her encounter with infant Jesus was about sixty years. She consistently and relentlessly found herself in the temple serving the Lord. This speaks volumes to her character.

Anna's character was impeccable. Character has to do with the mental and moral qualities distinctive to an individual. Moral character has to do with how you respond to a certain situation. Character is what comes out of you when extreme pressure is placed upon you. We can see from Scripture that Anna ran *into* the presence of God, not *from* His presence. It appears that she found strength and courage to persevere in faith in spite of her loss.

You might be saying in your heart, "Yes, that's good for Anna, but how can I overcome my situation?" I want to encourage you that everything starts with a decision. You must choose the way of the Lord. Turning to Him simply means focusing your attention on the promises in His Word and finding help in His presence.

God is raising up modern women who, resembling Anna, have walked through the fiery furnace and remained steadfast to the promises of God. God is enlisting His army of women who have persevered through many obstacles but still love Him with all of their hearts. These women are part of a special force with an assignment to pray until the glory of God covers the earth as the waters cover the sea.

I believe you are reading this book because you are called to be a modern-day Anna. You are armed with a resolve to obey the Lord no matter the cost. You are not afraid of the enemy or his tactics because you have seen the goodness of the Lord destroy the power of the enemy in your own life.

Just as Anna did, you must develop the art of waiting on the Lord. Scripture admonishes, "Those who wait upon the Lord shall renew their strength; they shall mount up with wings as eagles, they shall run and not be weary, and they shall walk and not faint" (Isa. 40:31). One of the major keys to developing character and displaying strength is waiting on the Lord. It is the key to victorious living. It is the key to displaying godly character. Waiting on the Lord involves serving, trusting, and expecting to see His goodness in your life.

We will explore the concept of waiting on the Lord more deeply in the next chapter. Now I want to talk to you about the final virtue I see in Anna's life: hope.

The Helmet of Hope

> Why are you cast down, O my soul? And why are you disquieted in me? Hope in God, for I will yet thank Him for the help of His presence. O my God, my soul is cast down within me; therefore I will remember You from the land of Jordan, and of the Hermon, from the hill of Mizar. Deep calls to deep at the noise of Your waterfalls; all Your waves and Your billows passed over me. Yet the Lord will command His lovingkindness in the daytime, and in the night His song will be with me, a prayer to the God of my life.
>
> —Psalm 42:5–8

Hope is an anointing that God likens to a helmet because it protects your mind (1 Thess. 5:8). It is also an anchor that causes your soul to be secure when waves of uncertainty hit your life (Heb. 6:19). Hope is the anchor for your soul, and it is rooted in the faithfulness of God. Another way to say this is that hope is a reservoir of strength for your mind, will, and emotions.

Hope is not wishful thinking—it is much more than that. The mind is Satan's battleground. Your emotions follow wherever your mind goes. Your thoughts, words, and emotions are deeply tied together. What you think and what comes out of your mouth greatly affect your emotional condition.

You can see from Psalm 42:5–8 that the soul can become very weary, confused, and filled with hopelessness. You must find hope in the face of God. You must be assured that in these times His face is toward you and that you are the object of His focus and loving care. He has promised to be with you both day and night.

You must be confident that God has a future and a hope for you. My favorite depiction of hope can be found in Hosea 2:15: "Then I will give her vineyards from there, and make the Valley of Achor a door of hope and expectation [anticipating the time when I will restore My favor on her]. And she will sing there and respond as in the days of her youth" (AMP). This scripture describes hope as a doorway to the future.

I believe that Anna found a door of hope to her future in the place of prayer and worship. When developed properly, hope paints a picture of the future for all of us. We can avoid unnecessary anguish and anxiety by deciding to let go of wrong thinking about our problems. Sometimes we can be so preoccupied asking "Why, God?" and "When, God?" that we never develop our faith. Many times we are consumed with trying to figure out the answers to all of life's problems. We must learn to trust that if God does not do it our way, His way is better.

It is in times of uncertainty that you must trust the heart of God for you, even when you don't understand His hand in your life. The hand of God speaks to His strategic dealings and plans for your future. Anna set an excellent example of having confidence in the heart of the Lord in the midst of crisis.

Jeremiah 29:11 says, "For I know the plans that I have for you, says the LORD, plans for peace and not for evil, to give you a future and a hope." This promise was spoken to Israel in the midst of great devastation. God is admonishing His people to not let the devastating situation of life determine their level of expectation. Anna must have followed this principle throughout her life.

Life is a process, not an event. If you fail today, if things fall apart, you can begin again. No matter what, it is never too late to start doing and believing the right things. It is never too late for a new beginning in your life. You must let go of painful setbacks, mistakes, failures, and wrong decisions to embrace the hope of a bright future. This is the hour to not let the disappointments, setbacks, and losses of life define your future. You must look at your life with eyes of hope and adopt God's point of view. You must find hope in Christ.

Prayers, Decrees, and Scriptures That Break Depression and Activate Hope

Lord, I believe that You will give me beauty for ashes. I receive strength instead of fear of the future. Lord, thank You for saturating my heart with the oil of gladness. I choose to put on the garment of praise instead of the spirit of mourning and heaviness. Your presence brings peace to my soul.

I break the spirit of hopelessness off of my life in the name of Jesus.

I choose to believe that I will see the goodness of the Lord in the land of the living.

I choose hope in the midst of life's hard situations.

I am an overcomer.

I will rejoice in hope.

I will have patience in testing and trials.

I will continue to relentlessly pray to the God of my salvation.

Rejoice in hope, be patient in suffering, persevere in prayer.

—ROMANS 12:12

Father, I believe that You love me and will take care of me as You promise in Your Word. I lift up my eyes of faith and look to You, the Author of my life. I cast my cares on You, for You care for me. I believe You will show up and take care of me. I am assured that You will not abandon me. I trust Your plans to give me the future I hoped for. Lord, fill my mind with Your thoughts toward me. I put on the helmet of hope. I shut down the voice of despair. Let my mind and heart be filled with Your precious thoughts for my life.

I'll show up and take care of you as I promised and bring you back home. I know what I'm doing. I have it all planned out—plans to take care of you, not abandon you, plans to give you the future you hope for.

—JEREMIAH 29:11, THE MESSAGE

God of hope, fill me with all joy and peace. I will trust in You with my whole heart, leaning not on my own understanding. I believe that I will abound in hope by the power of the Holy Ghost. I rebuke all feelings of hope deferred. I will not allow my heart to be weighed down and depressed. By faith I will lift up my voice and praise You. I believe that in the fullness of time my desires will be fulfilled. I will be strong and take heart because I put my hope in You, Lord.

Lord, You are close to the brokenhearted and save those who are crushed in spirit. I admit that I am disappointed. I come boldly without reservation or hesitation

*to Your throne to obtain mercy and find grace to help
in my time of need. I need Your grace to continue. Let
Your presence engulf me. Be my shield and exceedingly
great reward. I believe in Your saving, delivering power.
You are my Savior and will rescue me.*

Now may the God of hope fill you with all joy and peace
in believing, so that you may abound in hope, through
the power of the Holy Spirit.

—ROMANS 15:13

*I will not let the devil steal my expectation. I know that
surely there is a future for me, so my expectation will
not be cut off. I will not settle for less than what You
have promised me. I seize the hope that is set before me.
I trust in the Lord with all of my heart and lean not on
my own understanding. I will not allow my expectation
to be cut off by fear, doubt, unbelief, or time.*

For surely there is an end, and your expectation will not
be cut off.

—PROVERBS 23:18

The hope of the righteous will be gladness, but the
expectation of the wicked will perish.

—PROVERBS 10:28

Blessed is the man who trusts in the LORD, and whose
hope is the LORD.

—JEREMIAH 17:7

*Lord, my hope is in You! You are my Lord, my strength,
and the hope of my salvation. I trust Your Word. I am*

blessed and highly favored. Your banner over me is love.
I run into Your presence and I am safe.

But I will hope continually, and will praise You yet
more and more.

—Psalm 71:14, NKJV

O Israel, hope in the Lord; for with the Lord there is
mercy, and with Him is abundant redemption.

—Psalm 130:7, NKJV

Father, I will hope in You. I will live righteously and
serve You with the oil of gladness. I decree that every
wicked plot and plan against my life shall be cut off. I
cancel every wicked assignment against my life. I will
praise Your holy name forever. I partake of Your mer-
cies; they are new every morning. Your love never fails,
and Your mercy endures forever.

I am blessed because I put my trust in the Lord. I
will not trust in the arm of flesh because my hope, expec-
tation, and confidence is in You, my Lord. I will not let
my hope be cut off. I will hope continually in You.

I thank You, Lord, that You have mercy and grace
in Your heart for me. I will continually bless You and
praise You. Your Word is true. You cannot lie. You will
fulfill the desire of every living thing. Lord, I thank You
that You open Your hand and satisfy my desire.

But Christ is faithful over God's house as a Son, whose
house we are if we hold fast the confidence and the
rejoicing of our hope firm to the end.

—Hebrews 3:6

Lord, there are times when I feel I have no hope. Help me to hold fast to my confidence in You. Lord, give me the grace I need to persevere in the face of defeat.

So that by two unchangeable things [His promise and His oath] in which it is impossible for God to lie, we who have fled [to Him] for refuge would have strong encouragement and indwelling strength to hold tightly to the hope set before us. This hope [this confident assurance] we have as an anchor of the soul [it cannot slip and it cannot break down under whatever pressure bears upon it]—a safe and steadfast hope that enters within the veil [of the heavenly temple, that most Holy Place in which the very presence of God dwells].

—Hebrews 6:18–19, AMP

Father, because You cannot lie, I seize the hope that is set before me. I find refuge and strong encouragement in Your presence, and I find indwelling strength to hold tightly by prayer and praise to the hope that is set before me.

I believe Your Word. I thank You, Lord, that You are not like man. You cannot lie. You are a God of integrity. Every word You will bring to pass in my life, every promise. I trust Your love and Your character.

Your words are an anchor for my soul. You are my refuge and my fortress. I run to You and I am safe. I have an expectation that cannot be shaken. No matter what life tries to throw my way, You are my anchor. Your Word keeps me steadfast, unmovable, and abounding in Your love. I will wait for You and the fulfillment of Your words.

Therefore, prepare your minds for action, keep sober in spirit, fix your hope completely on the grace to be brought to you at the revelation of Jesus Christ.

—1 Peter 1:13, nasb

Chapter 2

LIVING A LIFE OF SACRIFICE

> And she was a widow of about eighty-four years of age who
> did not depart from the temple, but served God with fasting
> and prayer night and day.
>
> —LUKE 2:37

I'M INTRIGUED BY this scripture that says Anna did not depart from the temple but served the Lord with fasting and prayer day and night. What could make a woman never want to depart from the temple? Was it the exquisite decor? Was it that the temple attendants were kind to her and she felt safe and protected? Could it have been that her life was so desolate and lonely that she had nothing else to do? Maybe. However, I believe Anna was captivated by the presence of the Lord. She found her destiny waiting in the presence of the Lord. She found the pearl of great price and sold everything to buy it.

The Greek word for *served* in this passage means "one's extreme devotion and service to something he worships."[1] It depicts the service of the priesthood. This word also depicts someone serving God as the highest goal of his or her life. *Latreuō* implies giving undivided attention, living close to someone, and making your life a living sacrifice.[2] Those with an Anna anointing will intentionally place their lives in the close care of God. They will present their bodies as living sacrifices to God. They will surrender themselves and all that they are to God's plan and purpose for their lives.

A modern-day Anna will be fascinated by the love of God. Her prayers and fasting will not be duty based but motivated solely by being loved by God. God is love. His nature is love. He is the God of deep love and desire. The Lord is raising up modern-day women with the Anna anointing who will know His love and goodness. They will come seeking Him based on the confidence that He has loved them and will hear and act on their prayers.

God is challenging and changing all the misconceptions about prayer. One of the most common misconceptions about prayer is that all Christians are duty bound to pray—if you are going to be a good, God-fearing Christian, you need to pray every day. We have been given incorrect definitions and misrepresentations of the personality of God. God is not sitting on the throne with a black robe waiting to judge our imperfections. We've related to God as if He were a religious entity who is Lord over the universe only and not a loving Father. The picture painted by some is that God is distant and disinterested in the affairs of men, and we have to somehow persuade Him through fervent prayer to act on our behalf. Some teachers will give you the impression that God is just sitting on the throne looking down on lowly peasants, letting our world rapidly deteriorate, and we are running out of time. This type of mentality promotes fear-, shame-, and guilt-based prayers. Prayer empowers us to know Christ intimately. Prayer moves the hand of God to work intricately in our lives. It is the mechanism God has ordained to unlock His power and blessings in our lives. If you embrace the Anna anointing, you will be filled with the knowledge of His will and spiritual understanding to navigate life.

The modern-day Anna will be a woman whose heart has been captured by the love of God. She will be a woman who is rooted and grounded in the love of God. Ephesians 3:19 states that we should know the love of God. A woman with an Anna

anointing will intimately know the love of God. She will personally experience the transforming power of love. We cannot love
God with all our hearts until we know He loves us with all His
heart. When God wants to empower us to love Him, He reveals
Himself as One who loves us. "We love Him because [we understand that] He first loved us" (1 John 4:19). The modern-day Anna
will receive the reward of a lover, which is the power to love. The
Bible teaches that there is no greater love than to lay down your
life for a friend (John 15:13). A modern-day Anna will happily lay
aside the pleasures of life to labor with the Lord in intercession
for the nations.

The Divine Invitation

> Come to Me, all who are weary and heavily burdened
> [by religious rituals that provide no peace], and I will
> give you rest [refreshing your souls with salvation].
> Take My yoke upon you and learn from Me [following
> Me as My disciple], for I am gentle and humble in heart,
> and YOU WILL FIND REST (renewal, blessed quiet) FOR
> YOUR SOULS. For My yoke is easy [to bear] and My
> burden is light.
>
> —MATTHEW 11:28–30, AMP

I want to share with you my journey into discovering and walking
in the Anna anointing. It was March 3, 1991, a Sunday morning. I
can remember it clearly because it was one day after my twenty-
fifth birthday party when my then husband asked me for a
divorce. It was one of the most devastating moments of my life.
His actions came as a complete surprise to me. The night before
we were celebrating a milestone in my life with friends and family;
he had given me a surprise birthday party. We were working on
our second child, so I really thought we were happy. I thought

his declaration of getting a divorce was just a dream—maybe I didn't hear him correctly. He boldly proclaimed it again: "I want a divorce!" His words sent shock waves through my system—his voice reverberated through my nervous system releasing a spirit of fear through my entire being, and I was instantly ill. It felt as if someone snatched the rug from under my feet and left me sitting on my bottom trying to figure out which way was up.

I remember crying out to the Lord, "Why me? Why this? Why now?" I really loved being married. We had one child. I wanted her to grow up with her father in the house. We were planning and actively trying to have a little boy. I was the good Baptist girl who married a preacher's kid on Christmas Day. We taught Sunday school together. This was not supposed to be happening to me. After a series of events that happened in a span of three months, I found myself standing before a judge's bench and hearing a gavel slamming down on the desk as the judge declared the dissolution of my marriage. It felt as if my life was rapidly taking a nosedive out of my control, and at the sound of that gavel my life crashed headfirst to the ground. As I walked to the elevator, I heard a voice trumpet from heaven, "Come learn of Me!" I initially said to myself, "Devil, you will not drive me crazy. I cover my mind with the blood of Jesus!" Then I heard it again: "Come learn of Me!"

I soon realized that in the midst of heartbreak and devastation, the love of Father God was reaching out to me. The proclamation of "Come learn of Me" was filled with Spirit and life. The Lord was drawing me away by His Spirit from something temporal into something eternal. That proclamation reverberated through my entire being, releasing a peace that surpassed all my understanding. I was being called into the service of the Lord. I remember weeping bitterly and uncontrollably. I felt like a widow—it seemed as if my husband had died.

The end of my marriage activated a sense of loss with regard to my identity, security, and protection. But the end of my marriage also launched me on the greatest quest of my life. The Lord Jesus revealed to me the true riches of the kingdom. By the help of the Holy Spirit I began to set my heart on the Lord alone as the treasure beyond compare. Through prayer and meditation on the Word, my heart was set free of any inordinate desires or attachment to things that hindered me from freely giving all I had to the Lord in joy and gratitude for all that He had given to me. I found new joy and delight in the presence of the Lord. My heart experienced an awakening to the true lover of my soul.

Those with an Anna anointing will have a heart burning with love and desire for the Lord and His purposes. They will cultivate an intimate relationship with Lord, empowering them to be living flames of love to a lost generation. I had to learn the Lord was beckoning me to come away from all of the religious activities of my life and develop a real, personal relationship with Him. I thought doing enough religious activity would exempt me from destruction and loss. Jesus never promised that difficult, painful situations would not occur in our lives, but that if we come to Him in the place of prayer, we will find rest and refreshment for our souls. God doesn't cause death, divorce, or discouraging events to happen, but He uses them as a chain to link us to the good things to come. God will use ordinary events in our lives, whether wonderful or tragic, to move us toward our destiny. Those with an Anna anointing are women who understand that all things are working for their good.

Day after day His divine presence drew me to learn more about true love. I studied my Bible for hours, searching for significance. During this period in my life I scheduled everything around my devotional time with the Lord. I was becoming like Anna—all I wanted to do was to stay in the presence of the Lord day and night. The Lord, by the power of His love, had captured my heart, and I was His forever.

The Bible tells us that the Lord loves us with an everlasting love and draws us to Himself with lovingkindness (Jer. 31:3). The Lord invites us by the Holy Spirit to take up His yoke, for it is easy and His burden is light (Matt. 11:29–30). If you're going to be a modern-day Anna, you must take deliberate action to take up the yoke of the Lord. Matthew 11:29 states, "Take My yoke upon you." The word *take* in the Greek means "to deliberately lift or to deliberately take up."[3] A yoke is a wooden instrument that joins two animals together so they can combine their strength to pull a plow. Those with an Anna anointing will be yoked together with Jesus. A prayer life yoked together with Jesus makes the intercessor unbeatable. There is not a principality or demon that can stop the intercessor's prayer. A life that was once hard and full of anxiety and fear becomes pleasurable. Those with the Anna anointing understand what it means to partner with the Lord in prayer to bring about His plans and purpose for mankind on the earth.

Undivided Devotion

> I urge you therefore, brothers, by the mercies of God, that you present your bodies as a living sacrifice, holy, and acceptable to God, which is your reasonable service of worship.
>
> —ROMANS 12:1

Those with an Anna anointing will be women who have decided to become a living sacrifice unto the Lord. They will implement three foundational principles: presenting their bodies, abiding in Christ, and waiting on the Lord. Women with the Anna anointing will cultivate the art of presenting their bodies to the

Lord as a reasonable service. They will also learn how to abide in the presence of the Lord, letting His Word abide in them and asking for His heart and mind for our generation. They will develop the skill of waiting on the Lord to gain strength and longevity in the place of sustained intercession. These women will find that the key to power and authority is developing intimacy with the Lord.

Presenting your body

In Romans 12:1 the apostle Paul gives us a pattern on how to become a living sacrifice to God. The major key is found in the word *present*. In the Greek it means "to place beside; to place at one's disposal; to surrender; to offer, as to offer a sacrifice to God; or to present, as to present a special offering to God."[4] Presenting encompasses prayers of dedication and submission. It is a deliberate action of submitting your will to the will of the Lord. It is a solemn moment in your life in which you intentionally place yourself or humble yourself under the mighty hand of God. This is not a one-time action; an Anna will live in a continual state of consecration and surrender. Those with an Anna anointing train themselves to awaken each morning with a prayer of consecration in their hearts, submitting themselves to God's purposes.

Abiding in Christ

In John 15:7 Jesus says, "If you abide in Me, and My words abide in you, you will ask what you desire, and it shall be done for you" (NKJV). The modern-day Anna will cultivate the virtue of abiding in the presence of the Lord, making her prayers more effective. *Abide* is the Greek word *meno*, meaning "to stay, to remain, to continue, or to permanently abide in one place."[5] The word *meno* gives the idea that something is rooted, unmoving, and steadfast. We learn to abide in Christ by applying the Word of God to our everyday lives. We must look obediently to His

Word as the final authority in our lives. We must apply His promises to our hearts. Our hearts and desires are transformed into a life that bears fruit. Anna abided in the presence of the Lord. The Lord abides in our hearts progressively as He manifests His presence in our mind and emotions. Abiding in the Lord and His Word abiding in us give us authority in the spirit realm. True authority flows from love. Annas will have authority to bring about the will of the Lord on the earth.

Waiting on the Lord

Isaiah 40:31 (AMP) gives us a picture of the benefits of waiting on the Lord:

> But those who wait for the LORD [who expect, look for, and hope in Him] will gain new strength and renew their power; they will lift up their wings [and rise up close to God] like eagles [rising toward the sun]; they will run and not become weary, they will walk and not grow tired.

Those with an Anna anointing will gain new strength and endurance while waiting on the Lord in prayer. They wait with expectation and hope. This waiting implies an *active faith*. This is not the "pack your bags and wait until Jesus comes" faith! It is a faith that actively advances the gospel of the kingdom in expectation of revival. Anna waited in the presence of the Lord for sixty years before she saw the promise of the Messiah. She was a woman of great faith. She looked patiently, tarried, and hoped with great expectation, watching in prayer for the fulfillment of the promise.

The Hebrew word for *wait* in this passage is *qavah*. It means "to bind together (perhaps by twisting)" and "to be strong, robust."[6] Those with an Anna anointing will develop the art of waiting on the Lord through worship, prayer, and the study of the Word. Their hearts will become bound to the Lord. They will develop intimacy with the Lord through understanding the power of dwelling in His presence. They will become mighty women who understand the heart and mind of the Lord (1 Sam. 2:35).

"Lift up their wings like eagles" is a reference to soaring. *Soaring* means "rising above ordinary levels and gliding high in the air." Waiting will allow you to see life from God's perspective. Soaring is the ability to discern the direction of the wind of God through our heavenly experience or relationship with the Lord by waiting on Him. The eagle is said to be the only bird that can look directly into the sun. I believe those with an Anna anointing will develop a grace to look into the face of the Son, understanding His heart and mind with great accuracy through intercession for their generation. As we have said, Anna's name means "grace," and she was the daughter of a man whose name means "face of God." Anna's life pointed to the grace of looking into the face of God. Looking into the face of God refers to knowing the ways of God and not just the acts of God. Looking into the face of God symbolizes knowing God.

"Run and not become weary" speaks to Anna's ability to consistently and relentlessly pray day and night. Anna's fuel for prayer was found in the presence of the Lord. The modern-day Anna will be "strong in the Lord and in the power of His might" (Eph. 6:10). She will pray by the Spirit, not by the works of the flesh.

There will be times when the things you pray for may take a decade or even a lifetime to be fulfilled, but those with the Anna anointing will continue to wait in the presence of the Lord with a quiet trust. Even though Anna lost her husband at a young age, I believe she had the ability to wait in the presence of the Lord, trusting Him for healing, deliverance, and the fulfillment of His promises.

Anna cultivated the skill of waiting in her spirit, and that was how she waited in expectation to see the Messiah. Her spirit was alive and awake, anticipating the arrival of the Messiah. It could be said that Anna knew the exact time Jesus would come into the temple through prophetic insight, because as she waited in the presence of the Lord, He informed her, "It's time! Your promise is here!"

As I spent time waiting on the Lord regarding this book, He began to speak to me about His integrity and character. He spoke to my heart in that still, small voice that can ring so loudly with truth. He said, "Michelle, I am a God of great integrity. I do not lie. Every promise I've spoken over the lives of My people I am going to fulfill! I'm not playing games with your lives!" Many times the enemy will try to deceive us into thinking the Lord is disconnected from our lives, but that is a lie from the pit of hell. The faithfulness and love of God were tested and proven through Jesus Christ. We can boldly come to the throne of grace.

The key to becoming a modern-day Anna is cultivating and implementing the principles of presenting your body as a living sacrifice, abiding in Christ, and waiting on the Lord. All these things are rooted in trusting the character of the Lord. He is not like man—He cannot lie. You can safely trust Him when you surrender your entire life in service to Him.

Prayers of Presenting, Abiding, and Waiting

Lord, I present my body to You as a living sacrifice. I draw nigh to You with my entire heart. I give myself to You. I want to be holy and acceptable to You. My life is in Your hands. I give You my heart and all of my pains and disappointments. Create in me a clean heart, and renew a right, steadfast spirit within me. Lord, take me

to the mount of change. I want to be transformed into
Your image. Make me like You. Show me why You created me.

I believe Your Word. You are the vine, and I am
the branch. I abide and remain in You all of the days
of my life. Without You I can do nothing. I need You
and Your presence in my life. Lead me and guide me by
Your Spirit. I want to have fruit that remains in my life.
I want to have godly character as I abide in You. Show
me Your ways. Lead me in the path of righteousness for
Your name's sake.

I will wait for You, Jesus. You're the strength of my
life. Lord, I ask that You renew my strength as the
eagle's. Let this be a season of refreshing and renewal
in my life. I believe that You give power to the weak
and to those who have no might, You increase strength.
I receive Your divine empowerment in my life. I break
all discouragement and weakness from my life. I decree
that I am strong in the Lord and in the power of His
might! I will not be weary, nor will I faint! I look to the
hills from which comes my help. My help comes from
the Lord!

Chapter 3

THE PROPHETESS

I have set watchmen on your walls, O Jerusalem; they shall
never hold their peace day or night. You who make mention
of the LORD, do not keep silent, and give Him no rest till He
establishes and till He makes Jerusalem a praise in the earth.

—ISAIAH 62:6–7, NKJV

HEAVEN IS READY to invade the earth with undeniable power
as in the days of the Book of Acts. There is a great awakening
on the horizon filled with glorious revival. This revival will not
happen in a vacuum. Prayer must precede revival.

In Isaiah 62:6–7 those who make mention of the Lord are
the prophetic intercessors God is raising up on the earth. The
phrase *make mention* is key in describing the function of those
with an Anna anointing. *Make mention* comes from the Hebrew
word *zachar*. It means "to remember, bring into mind, recollect;
also, to mention, meditate upon, mark down, record, recall, and
retain in one's thoughts."[1] The special company of women with
the Anna anointing will take hold of the altar of God in prayer,
reasoning with the Lord and reminding Him of His promises for
mankind. I believe Anna was the beginning of the fulfillment of
this prophetic promise. There is a generation of women who will
fast and pray, preparing the way for the glory and power of the
Lord to come on the earth.

Prayer is the primary way God has chosen to release His power
on the earth. The prophetess Anna's primary assignment was in

the temple or house of God. She was an intercessory prophetess. Through her fasting and prayers she helped prepare the way for the coming of the Lord. I believe she represented the wise virgins in Matthew 25—she had her lamp trimmed, burning, and filled with oil of the Spirit. She was not sleeping or slumbering—she set up a prayer vigil, and she paid a price. Her praying day and night represented the power of the watch of the Lord. It represents relentless, urgent prayer. Those with the Anna anointing will understand the power of praying in the day and praying in the night. We will discuss this principle in the next chapter.

God is awakening a company of women akin to Anna once again. This is a season in history in which extreme prayer is needed to bring the glory of God on the earth. The Lord is setting watchmen on the wall to cry out in desperation for God to visit our churches, change society, and deliver and set free those in captivity. God is raising up an Anna company who will have the anointing to see in the spirit and in the Scripture, pinpointing what God is about to do on the earth. This enables them to understand God's divine times and to proclaim them to those who look for salvation.

What Is Prophetic Intercession?

> But if they are prophets, and if the word of the LORD is with them, let them now make intercession to the LORD of hosts, that the vessels which are left in the house of the LORD, in the house of the king of Judah, and at Jerusalem, do not go to Babylon.
>
> —JEREMIAH 27:18, NKJV

The term *intercession* has several meanings. In this section I want to take a look at the word used in the New Testament. The apostle Paul used the Greek word *enteuxis*, which means "a prayer with a set meeting time, place, and purpose" and "to mediate or to stand in for another."[2] It can also mean "a petition to a king," in the sense of going before the king to make a request of him. It implies that prophetic intercessors have intimate access to and fellowship with the King of kings. Through prayer we have both privilege and power. "It is not that prayer itself has the power, but that we have access to the One who has the power."[3]

Prophetic intercession is the infusion of the priestly and the prophetic. In the simplest form prayer is talking to God, and prophecy is declaring what He has said about a subject. Prophetic intercession combines the office of the priest with the office of the prophet. The priest worships, has fellowship with, and ministers to God, and the prophet speaks for God to the people. Prophetic intercession originates in the mind of God. It is a type of prayer that is inspired by the Holy Spirit. It is expressed when the Holy Spirit quickens your human spirit by providing particular scriptures for you to apply to the matter at hand, an urgent need on the heart of God. When there is a set time to birth a promise of God on the earth, God drops a burden on a prophetic intercessor. This type of praying is a fusion of God's revelation and insights into what needs to be prayed and how to pray. God will direct you to pray to bring forth His will on the earth as it is in heaven. The prophetic intercessor must wait before God with an awakened ear to hear His voice, spiritual eyes to see, and a receptive, sensitive heart to receive God's burden.

Traits of a Prophetic Intercessor

> But as it is written, "Eye has not seen, nor ear heard, nor has it entered into the heart of man the things which God has prepared for those who love Him." But God

> has revealed them to us by His Spirit. For the Spirit
> searches all things, yes, the deep things of God.
>   —1 CORINTHIANS 2:9–10

Prophetic intercessors need to be filled with the Holy Spirit to receive revelation from the heart of God. Prophetic intercessors must have an intimate relationship with the Holy Spirit. Notice Paul begins this verse by stating man's inability in the natural realm to understand the deep things of God. The word *search* denotes the process of investigation. The Holy Spirit searches and investigates the deep, predetermined plans of God for each individual, city, or nation.

The Holy Spirit reveals these plans and purposes of God to our spirits. The word *reveal* comes from a Greek word that means "to uncover, [unveil], or disclose; to make known, make manifest."[4] It is a picture of something suddenly being removed and bringing obscure things into plain sight. When the Holy Spirit lifts the veil from your spiritual eyes, ears, and heart, you can perceive truth that was veiled from your understanding. This is called revelation. *Revelation* is defined as "the act of disclosing or discovering to others what was before unknown to them; appropriately, the disclosure or communication of truth to men by God himself, or by his authorized agents, the prophets and apostles."[5]

Revelation must be interpreted correctly before it is applied. The prophetic word or revelation comes through three basic spiritual senses: the ears, the eyes, and the heart. The Lord give us the ability to hear His voice, opens our eyes to see from His perspective, and touches our hearts to feel as He does.

Prophetic intercessors need awakened ears. They need ears open to the Holy Spirit, which allows their hearts to comprehend. Just as we have natural senses, we also have parallel spiritual senses. The Lord by the power of the Holy Spirit will open the ear of the prophetic intercessor. Isaiah 50:4–5 states, "He awakens me morning by morning; He awakens my ear to listen as the learned. The Lord God has opened my ear." The Lord Jesus frequently admonished, "He who has ears to hear, let him hear" (e.g., Matt. 11:15). The Old Testament word for *hear* or *listen* is *shama'*, meaning "to listen; to obey; discern; perceive."[6] Prophetic intercessors are gifted by the Holy Spirit to discern the will of God, to perceive the accurate time to declare through prayer and intercession the promises of God for a people, a city, or a nation. Prophetic intercessors must have their spiritual ears attuned to the voice of the Lord to hear instructions on what prayer is needed for specific situations. Prophetic intercessors have to be awakened to hear the voice of the Lord so that we may have the tongue of the learned to speak and pray His wisdom and comfort our generation (Isa. 50:4).

Prophetic intercessors need vision and spiritual sight. Vision is the matrix of prophecy. Prophecy is the speaking forth of that which one sees and hears in the realm of the spirit; it is the articulation of the visions of God. The ministry of prophecy should always build up the church's faith in God and the Lord Jesus Christ by articulating the vision of the Lord. This enlarges the people's understanding of His greatness. Prophetic intercessors are given eyes to see from a heavenly perspective. Through the gift of discerning of spirits they can see what no one else can see. Prophetic intercessors have an anointing from God that causes scales to be removed from their eyes so they can see the invisible. They give insight into spiritual issues, causing us to see that there are more with us than against us.

> Then Elisha prayed, "Lord, open his eyes and let him see." So the Lord opened the eyes of the young man, and he saw that the mountain was full of horses and chariots of fire surrounding Elisha.
>
> —2 Kings 6:17

The prophetic intercessor needs an understanding, listening heart. Solomon had greatness of understanding and largeness of heart. Largeness of heart is the ability to perceive—the ability to understand beginning, middle, and end of a situation all at once. The Lord gave him a supernatural ability to see the whole picture (1 Kings 4:29). The prophetic intercessor is given the supernatural ability to observe the affairs of men from the eternal realm.

> He also has planted eternity in men's hearts and minds [a divinely implanted sense of a purpose working through the ages which nothing under the sun but God alone can satisfy].
> —ECCLESIASTES 3:11, AMPC

Solomon also asked for an understanding heart: "Give Your servant therefore an understanding heart to judge Your people, that I may discern between good and bad" (1 Kings 3:9). In this passage "understanding heart" is sometimes translated as "listening heart," meaning a heart that listens to God to accomplish what He has assigned. This is the call of the prophetic intercessor.

In addition to the spiritual senses, the prophetic intercessor needs spiritual discernment. Spiritual discernment gives one the ability to know and be informed of what is in the spiritual realm. The gift of discerning of spirits is supernatural insight into the realm of the spirit. *Discern* means to separate out or to reveal truth. It can also mean "to detect with senses other than vision."[7] Spiritual discernment is not suspicious. It reveals the type of spirit behind a person, situation, action, or message. It is supernatural revelation in the spirit concerning the source, nature, and activity of any spirit. Many prophetic intercessors have the gift of discerning of spirits.

> But the natural man does not receive the things of the Spirit of God, for they are foolishness to him; nor can he know them, because they are spiritually discerned.
>
> —1 Corinthians 2:14

The Greek word for *discerned* is *anakrino*, meaning "to distinguish, or separate out so as to investigate (*krino*) by looking throughout (*ana*, intensive) objects or particulars...to examine, scrutinize, question, to hold a preliminary judicial examination."[8] First Corinthians 12:10 states that there is a gift of discerning of spirits, implying that more than one spirit can be in operation. The gift of discerning of spirits activates your perception, giving you grace to see what others cannot see. There are four types of spirits that the prophetic intercessor can encounter during times of prayer:

1. The Holy Spirit—The intercessor must discern the movement and manifestation of the Holy Spirit. The Holy Spirit manifests as the dove at times and as tongues of fire at others. There will be times in corporate gatherings of prayer and intercession that the prophetic intercessor will need to discern what the Holy Spirit is doing and whom He wants to move through. It is important that intercessors discern the purposes and plan of the Holy Spirit, letting personal agendas and ideologies die.

2. Demonic spirits—Evil spirits like to follow intercessors to prayer. One major spirit is the demonic spirit of divination. Acts 16:16–18 gives us a clear example of how it takes the gift of discerning of spirits to recognize evil spirits in operation: "On one occasion, as we went to the place of prayer, a servant girl possessed

with a spirit of divination met us, who brought her masters much profit by fortune-telling. She followed Paul and us, shouting, 'These men are servants of the Most High God, who proclaim to us the way of salvation.' She did this for many days. But becoming greatly troubled, Paul turned to the spirit and said, 'I command you in the name of Jesus Christ to come out of her.' And it came out at that moment."

Notice in this passage this young girl proclaimed the truth about Paul, but the motivation was evil. Evil spirits can speak a partial truth to bring greater deception at a later time. Paul, by the gift of discerning of spirits, was grieved and perceived that it was an evil spirit operating through the young girl.

3. Human spirits—In order to be effective intercessors for mankind, we need to see men from God's perspective. "Man looks on the outward appearance, but the LORD looks on the heart" (1 Sam. 16:7). Jesus was not fooled or deceived by people. John 2:23–25 states: "Now when He was in Jerusalem at the Passover Feast, many believed in His name when they saw the signs which He did. But Jesus did not entrust Himself to them, because He knew all men, and did not need anyone to bear witness of man, for He knew what was in man." The gift of discerning of spirits will allow you to know what is inside man. You will not be deceived by outward behavior modification. God will allow you to see the crooked, wrong motivations of human beings and pray to see change in their lives.

4. Angelic spirits—Scripture is clear about the activity of angels in the affairs of mankind. Elisha, through

the gift of discerning of spirits, saw that there were
more fighting with him than against him (2 Kings
6:17). Prophetic intercessors may be given eyes to see
the angels battling on our behalf.

Prophetic intercessors need to understand the Word of God.
Scripture tells us Anna did not depart from the temple, which
implies she heard the reading of God's Word and the proclamations about Christ. Thus it was easy to recognize Him when He
arrived. Prophetic intercessors must be filled with the Word of
God. It is out of the knowledge of the written Word that prophetic intercession actually flows. The Holy Spirit quickens the
Logos Word to our spirit man, making it a *rhema* word for the
situation. Prophetic intercession is a combination of the written
Word of God and the voice of the Lord. It does not come from
your mind—it comes from the Holy Spirit. Prophetic intercession takes hold of heaven's agenda and releases it on earth.

Prophetic intercessors also need a heart of compassion.
Compassion is love in action. *Compassion* means "a feeling of
deep sympathy and sorrow for another who is stricken by misfor-
tune, accompanied by a strong desire to alleviate the suffering."[9]
The Greek word for *compassion* is *splanchnizomai*, meaning "'to
be moved with deep compassion or pity.' The Greeks regarded
the bowels (*splanchna*) as the place where strong and powerful
emotions originated. The Hebrews regarded *splanchna* as the
place where tender mercies and feelings of affection, compassion, sympathy, and pity originated."[10] Compassion is a key element of prophetic intercession. This virtue allows the intercessor
to feel and act passionately with great urgency in prayer to alleviate suffering. Compassion is the motivation behind identification intercession.

Modern-day women with the Anna anointing will be equipped
with the traits of a prophetic intercessor. These spiritual gifts

will empower them to use their spiritual senses to heighten their understanding, to discern the presence of the Holy Spirit, to identify intentions and motivations in the human heart, and to perceive the activity of evil spirits, causing them to be effective prophetic intercessors with hearts of compassion. They will be women who understand the power of praying the Word of God with great compassion for humanity.

Learn to Discern the Burden of the Lord

> But solid food belongs to those who are of full age, that is, those who by reason of use have their senses exercised to discern both good and evil.
> —HEBREWS 5:14, NKJV

To be an effective prophetic intercessor, you must learn to discern the burden of the Lord. The greatest key to being a prophetic intercessor is your relationship to the Lord. You will become what you behold. Second Corinthians 3:18 says, "But we all, seeing the glory of the Lord with unveiled faces, as in a mirror, are being transformed into the same image from glory to glory by the Spirit of the Lord." Those with the Anna anointing will be separated, consecrated ones who learn to practice the presence of the Lord. They will be filled with the Spirit, learning to discern the heart of Jesus for this generation.

Here are some keys to developing the prophetic intercessor in you. If you are a born-again believer, there may be times when the Lord is prompting you to pray or turn your attention to a particular matter on the earth. Hebrews 5:14 alerts us to the fact that we must have our spiritual sense exercised to discern between good and evil. We are the sheep of the Lord, and there is grace to hear His voice confidently.

God speaks to our human spirit, so usually the leading and

prompts from Him sound like our inner voice. We can have a hard time distinguishing between our human voice, the voice of the Lord, and the voice of Satan. This is why we must have our spiritual sense exercised. I cannot manipulate the activity of the Holy Spirit, but I can give you some keys to recognizing and responding to the Holy Spirit's promptings in your life. We must understand that God has many ways to communicate His burden to His intercessors. We are His sheep, and we hear His voice. God speaks in a still, small voice.

God will speak something to bless the body of Christ. God's first command was to bring light to chaos (Gen. 1:3). God speaks as a means to bring life and order. Prophetic intercessors should pray with the intention to release the light to every dark situation. I believe that modern-day women with the Anna anointing have the ability to release an unprecedented amount of the power and blessing of the Lord upon the earth.

Burdens from the Lord can come in many different forms. Many times the Lord will have me, as a prophetic intercessor, watch television or read a news article to gain knowledge of what is happening in the city. I have received the burden of the Lord just from hearing other people's plights. The burden of the Lord can be described as an awakening in your spirit to the heart and desire of the Lord. It is a heaviness or weight. In this context the Lord will alert you, as an intercessor, to His heart for a situation to pray for His answer or solution to help the human condition, something you have no knowledge of in the natural. When you pray the will of God, the prompt or heaviness lifts, and you can go back to your normal life activities. Many prophets and intercessors fall into a pit of the devil and carry around false burdens. They let the original God-given burden move them over into the soulish realm instead of keeping it in the spirit. Jesus said, "My yoke is easy, and My burden is light" (Matt. 11:30). We must position ourselves as prophetic intercessors and mediators between heaven and earth to receive the burden of the Lord for our generation.

We can ask for prayer assignments. First Samuel 2:35 states, "And I will raise up for Myself a faithful priest; what is in My heart and in My soul he will do it. And I will build him a sure house, and it will walk before My anointed forever." Do not be afraid to initiate conversation with the heavenly Father because of fear of deception or demonic interference. Many with an Anna anointing will be connected to the heart and mind of the Lord. They will understand by the spirit of revelation the secrets of the Lord. In Matthew 7:7–11 Jesus states that if you ask the Father for gifts, He will not give you something contrary to what you ask. God our Father, who is so in love with human beings, loves to hear the sound of a human voice asking and inquiring of Him. Jeremiah 33:3 says, "Call to Me, and I will answer you, and show you great and mighty things which you do not know." *Mighty* comes from the Hebrew word *batsar*, which means "secrets, mysteries, inaccessible things." [11] The modern-day Anna needs to ask, seek, and knock, and God will answer.

Focus is key to recognizing and responding to the leading of the Spirit. When you receive an impression from the Lord in a thought picture, ask yourself, "What do I see, feel, or have a knowing about regarding the situation?" (See Isaiah 21:3–4.) God speaks through your spirit. It sounds like you.

God will often quicken one sentence, word, picture, or thought to your spirit. Then you must exercise your faith to pray about the revelation given. It is like a piece of string on a sweater. Give it one pull, and let the words flow. Open your mouth wide, and God will fill it (Ps. 81:10). The Holy Spirit will not move your mouth or override your will. You must give voice and yield to what He is nudging you to pray.

One of the greatest privileges given to mankind is the honor of colaboring with the God of the universe. Prayer closets and prayer gatherings are the governmental centers of the earth. The Lord has extended an invitation for women to partner with Him to release divine intervention in the affairs of men. Our prayer moves the hand of God. Our prayer engages heaven's actions. There is readiness to answer prayer in the heart of God. (See Isaiah 65:24.)

Prayers of the Prophetic Intercessor

Lord, give me a piece of Your heart for my generation. Help me to be a woman of compassion. Break my heart with things that break Your heart. Take away my stony heart and give me a heart of flesh. God, I repent of all hardness of heart that makes me indifferent to the plight of men. Father, I pray that You will make me sensitive to the moving of the Holy Spirit. Your Word says that manifestation of the Spirit is given to each one. I ask that You give me the gift of discerning of spirits. Enlighten the eyes of my understanding. Remove every scale from my eyes that I may see by Your Spirit. Awaken my ear so I might hear and perceive what You are saying and doing. I break off all blind, deaf, and dumb spirits. I will be a woman who hears Your voice. Make me a woman of vision and insight. Lord, empower me to pray effective, fervent prayer. Make me a house of prayer for all nations!

But if they are prophets, and if the word of the LORD is with them, let them now make intercession to the LORD of Hosts, that the vessels which are left in the house of

the LORD and in the house of the king of Judah and in
Jerusalem not go to Babylon.

—JEREMIAH 27:18

As I mentioned in the introduction, the spirit of Babylon has
infiltrated our culture with mixture and confusion. This spirit
plots to build a city or culture without honoring God. (See
Genesis 11:4.) The spirit of Babylon wants to exercise power and
spiritual experience without the Lord Jesus. This spirit opposes
the absolute truth of Scripture and releases confusion in the
identity of human beings. Here is an example of an intercessory
prayer against the spirit of Babylon:

> I bind the activity of the spirit of Babylon. I bind the
> spirit of confusion attacking the mind and identity of
> a generation. I loose the love and truth of the Word of
> God. I bind every antichrist spirit attacking this gen-
> eration. I break every spirit of hardness of heart form-
> ing in a generation of people. Lord, I cry out for a great
> awakening of human hearts. Lord, raise up a genera-
> tion of passionate preachers who will preach Your Word
> with power and demonstration. Let the miracles, signs,
> and wonders be released that will cause men to turn
> back to You. I pray that You will release confusion into
> every agenda that stands against the Lord Jesus Christ.
> Lord, raise up modern-day people like Daniel, Shadrach,
> Meshach, and Abed-Nego who will not bow to the spirit
> of Babylon but will have courage to worship the true
> and living God!

Chapter 4

THE WATCHMAN/PROPHET

Go, station a watchman; let him declare what he sees.

—ISAIAH 21:6

SCRIPTURE DECLARES THAT Anna was a prophetess. A prophetess is a female prophet. A prophet is someone who has an anointing to know the heart and mind of God. A prophet watches over the word of the Lord for the current generation and prays it into existence. Anna prayed night and day, watching for the arrival of the Messiah. She was a watchman-type prophet. She served the Lord with prayer night and day as a watchman. She set up a vigil in the presence of the Lord. There is a company of women akin to Anna arising who will watch and pray for a visitation of the Lord upon the earth.

A prophet also has the power and authority to speak forth by decree and proclamation the predetermined purposes for the earth. Scripture does not give details of how Anna prayed, but it does say when she prayed. An army of women intercessors are rising up who will set up a watch of prayer around the promises of God. The Greek word for *watch* means "be vigilant, wake, be watchful."[1] A modern-day Anna will function as a watchman on the wall. She will carefully watch and wait in the presence of the Lord to receive His instructions for this generation. According to James W. Goll, "A watchman also warns the city far in advance when an enemy approaches. He sounds an alarm to awaken the people because he knows 'to forewarn them is to alert and arm them.'" [2] When Anna witnessed the Messiah in the temple, she began to alert those who looked for salvation that their deliverer had come to the earth. The modern-day Anna will empower many to find their places in the army of God. She will show many the way of salvation through her teaching and preaching, snatching many from the mouth of hell and the grave.

Watch can be defined as "to keep vigil as a devotional exercise; to be awake during the night; to keep guard." [3] This is the job of modern-day women with the Anna anointing. They will patrol in the spirit with asking, seeking, and knocking prayers to declare to the church the time and season in which we are living. They will protect the church from plots and traps of the enemy through their prayers and decree.

Watching implies responsible involvement. Watchmen were both caretakers and guardians in biblical times. Some were assigned to protect crops from predators and thieves; some were assigned to protect cities from military invasion. Watchmen were to be proactive in their role as guardians. They were vigilant. There were watches around the clock. Watchmen were vocal; they warned of danger with shouts or trumpets. [4] These are the days when the Lord is stirring the hearts of women to be involved in the destiny of a generation. God will use us to set up watches to protect God's people. We will guard with our prayers, warn with our preaching, and protect with our prophesying. Through the grace of watching and praying night and day we will shape the destiny of nations.

The words for *watch* used in the Bible have implications for spiritual watchfulness. Here are some examples:

+ *shaqad*—to be alert; to be on the lookout (either for good or [evil]); to keep watch of, be wakeful over [5]

Blessed is the man who hears me, watching daily at my gates, waiting at the posts of my doors.

—PROVERBS 8:34

✦ *shomrah*—to watch for the purpose of restraint [6]

Set a watch, O LORD, before my mouth; keep the door of my lips.

—PSALM 141:3, KJV

✦ *nēphō*—to be sober, to be calm and collected in spirit; to be temperate, dispassionate, circumspect [7]

But the end of all things is at hand: be ye therefore sober, and watch unto prayer.

—1 PETER 4:7, KJV

Anna was a prophet who tapped into an eternal strategy. She learned the power of praying night and day. She prayed in the time frames the Lord prescribed in Scripture. Prayer watches in the first-century church were a part of normal Christian life. These prayer watches were designed to maintain the practice of offering God a continual sacrifice of praise and prayer. In the early church every committed Christian was expected to devote time in prayer at a specific time.

The Eight Watches

We must be strategic to pray the right prayer during the right time of day. Lamentations 2:19 gives us a picture of the heart and assignment of those with an Anna anointing: "Arise, cry out in the night, at the beginning of the watches; pour out your heart like water before the face of the Lord. Lift your hands to Him for the lives of your young children, who faint for hunger at the head of every street." Women akin to Anna will share in God's heart for others, arising out of slumber and indifference. This is the season to shake ourselves out of hardness of heart and cry out for the church and for the nations. We must guard this generation from the schemes of the enemy and birth them into revival. We must lift up our hands and cry out night and day for our children. There are specific spiritual dynamics associated with certain watches, or time periods. There are eight watches—four night watches and four day watches, covering twenty-four hours—and each has a spiritual significance.

First watch (6:00 p.m. to 9:00 p.m.)

This is a time of meditation and self-evaluation. During this watch the sun is setting. According to Jewish tradition it is the end of the old day and the beginning of the new day. This is a time of humbling yourself under the mighty hand of God, allowing the Lord to search your heart. This is a time of repentance and realigning your heart with the purposes of the Lord. This is also a time of being strengthened with might through His Spirit in the inner man. This is the time to quiet your soul and ask the Lord to remove any distractions from your heart.

The evening watch is also a time to get focused on your future. During this watch you can pray for your future provision and blessings. The evening watch was also the time Jesus chose to inaugurate the new covenant (Matt. 26:20–30). The evening watch is time for consecration and dedication to Lord. In this watch we can appropriate the blessings of God's covenant and ask Him to manifest those blessing into our lives. During this time the Lord will also speak to you concerning His heart and mind regarding your prayer assignment.

Second watch (9:00 p.m. to midnight)

This is the time to set up a canopy of praise and worship over your life. Psalm 119:62 says, "At midnight I will rise to give thanks to You, because of Your righteous judgments." During this watch, through prayer and praise we can release the judgment of God into situations upon the earth. It was at the midnight hour that Paul and Silas gave thanks to the Lord, resulting in prison doors being opened and captives being set free (Acts 16:25–26). This is the time when angels are released on our behalf. This can also be a time of visitation and supernatural happenings of God.

Third watch (midnight to 3:00 a.m.)

This time is known as "the witching hour," a time witches try to control and take advantage of. It is a time when witchcraft is used to plant the seeds of the enemy and hijack this time from God and His people. It is not a time for novices in the area of spiritual warfare. This watch requires stable, disciplined, well-trained intercessors. This is a time to "intercede and take back from the enemy the authority that he has attempted to steal."[8]

Fourth watch (3:00 a.m. to 6:00 a.m.)

It was during the fourth watch that Jesus walked on water (Matt. 14:25–33). This is the watch when we can see divine intervention in our lives. During this watch you can declare the lordship of Jesus on the earth. Jesus was exercising His dominion and authority over creation when He walked on water and spoke to the winds. This is the watch when you can declare the mercies of the Lord over your life and those in your sphere of influence. This is the time when God will give you faith and courage to step out and follow Him, even in the face of adversity. This watch is when you begin to declare the newness of God in your life: new mercies, new favor, and new grace. This is the time to declare that wisdom and revelation are your portion. This is the watch when you command your morning and order your day (Job 38:12–13). This is the watch when you speak to the storms of life. The Bible tells us, "Death and life are in the power of the tongue" (Prov. 18:21). Based on Job 38, we can use our prayers to shake wickedness out of our days and command our mornings. This is the watch to declare the promises of God.

Fifth watch (6:00 a.m. to 9:00 a.m.)

This watch is considered the prime watch, the first watch of the day. This is a time to order your steps and consecrate yourself and your day to the will of God. As it is written, "Order my steps according to Your word, and let not any iniquity have dominion over me" (Ps. 119:133), and "Consecrate yourselves today to the LORD, that He may bestow a blessing on you this day" (Exod. 32:29).

Sixth watch (9:00 a.m. to noon)

During this watch the Holy Spirit was poured out upon the disciples (Acts 2:1–21). The third hour of the day was about 9:00 a.m. This is very significant because the number nine represents the gifts and fruits of the Holy Spirit. The Israelites used this as a time for corporate prayer. This was also the daily time of prayer and instruction at the temple.[9] During this watch we should pray for the power and character of the Holy Spirit to be released in the church and upon the church and its leaders. This is the time to pray for the mighty unseen power of the Holy Spirit to be released upon all nations. During this watch you can pray for revival and spiritual awakening.

Seventh watch (noon to 3:00 p.m.)

Historically this watch is when Jesus Christ was dying on the cross and completely identified with the sin of humanity, atoning for the sins of the world and bringing redemption and restoration. During this watch you can pray that God would redeem the time and restore the years lost in your life. Midday is also the time when the sun is brightest and hottest. During this watch you can pray for wisdom and revelation. Rebuke every spirit of darkness. Decree that the path of your destiny will shine with every rising hope and promise.

Midday is also the time to pray Psalm 91 because of the destruction that comes at noonday. During this season in human history, Psalm 91 should be confessed over your life and the lives of those in your sphere of influence.

Below you will find key points taken from Psalm 91 (AMP) that should be prayed every day:

> He who dwells in the shelter of the Most High will remain secure and rest in the shadow of the Almighty [whose power no enemy can withstand].
>
> —PSALM 91:1

We must declare our position in prayer. Dwelling under the shadow of the Most High is done by prayer and worship. This will develop an ark of safety and protection.

> I will say of the LORD, "He is my refuge and my fortress, my God, in whom I trust [with great confidence, and on whom I rely]!"
>
> —PSALM 91:2

The promises of God are voice activated. There is power in confession. You must declare who the Lord is to you daily.

> For He will save you from the trap of the fowler, and from the deadly pestilence.
>
> —PSALM 91:3

We can cancel every plan of darkness against our lives through prayer. A trap is hidden from its prey. It can catch you unawares. Praying this prayer will reveal things not known in the natural. Praying this will give you foresight into the wicked plans of the enemy and a prophetic advantage to defeat and utterly destroy him.

> He will cover you and completely protect you with His pinions, and under His wings you will find refuge…
> —Psalm 91:4

His faithfulness is a shield and a wall.

> You will not be afraid of the terror of night, nor of the arrow that flies by day…
> —Psalm 91:5

The spirit of terror has blanketed our land. With ISIS and terrorist cells in our nation, we must bind the works of terrorism and decree that the Lord will frustrate all of their plans and catch them in their craftiness (Job 5:12–13). We must pray for divine intelligence for those responsible for our security and that every terrorist cell will be uncovered in our land. We must also pray against gun violence in our streets. Decree that a bullet will never penetrate your body or the bodies of your loved ones.

> Nor of the pestilence that stalks in darkness, nor of the destruction (sudden death) that lays waste at noon.
> —Psalm 91:6

Plead the blood of Jesus against premature death and destruction. God told Moses to put the blood of the lamb on the doorposts so when the death angel passed by, the people of Israel would be protected. This is a season when we must appropriate the blood of Jesus over our lives, cities, and nations.

> A thousand may fall at your side and ten thousand at
> your right hand, but danger will not come near you.
> —Psalm 91:7

The heart of an intercessor is to pray for mercy and protection. It can be heartbreaking to see people perish, so rise up and pray and fight for life, realizing the painful reality is that some will perish.

> You will only [be a spectator as you] look on with your
> eyes and witness the [divine] repayment of the wicked
> [as you watch safely from the shelter of the Most High].
> Because you have made the Lord, [who is] my refuge,
> even the Most High, your dwelling place,...
> —Psalm 91:8–9

This verse tells us we must make the Lord our refuge and dwelling place. We can make the Lord our dwelling place by praying and decreeing the Word of God every day, creating a canopy of protection.

> No evil will befall you, nor will any plague come near
> your tent.
> —Psalm 91:10

With the breakout of plagues such as SARS, bird flu, and Ebola, we must decree the healing protection of God. This passage promises protection from sickness and disease as a blessing of the redeemed life.

> For He will command His angels in regard to you, to
> protect and defend and guard you in all your ways [of
> obedience and service].
> —Psalm 91:11

The way to activate angels is to decree the Word of God. Angels listen to the Word of God that proceeds from your mouth. We are not to command or order angels around. Only proclaiming the written Word of God will cause angels to move (Ps. 103:20).

> They will lift you up in their hands, so that you do not [even] strike your foot against a stone. You will tread upon the lion and cobra; the young lion and the serpent you will trample underfoot.
>
> —PSALM 91:12–13

Through the power of binding and loosing, declaring and decreeing the Word of God, and pleading the blood of Jesus, we tread upon the enemies of our soul.

> Because he set his love on Me, therefore I will save him; I will set him [securely] on high, because he knows My name [he confidently trusts and relies on Me, knowing I will never abandon him, no, never].
>
> —PSALM 91:14

Here the scripture begins to change from instructions to promises. God responds to the prayer, giving assurance of presence and protection. It is so important to keep your attention and focus on who God is and how much He loves us. We must turn our attention to Him, magnifying and exalting Him about life's difficulties. We must know the name of God and pray and declare it throughout the earth. He is Almighty God. There is power in praying the names of God. When you proclaim His name, He shows up in the nature of His name.

> He will call upon Me, and I will answer him; I will be with him in trouble; I will rescue him and honor him.
>
> —PSALM 91:15

I love the word *call* in this passage. It's the Hebrew *qara'*, meaning "to cry out; utter a loud sound; to call unto, cry (for help), call (with name of God)."[10] If you call on Him as your deliverer, He will deliver you. If you call on Him as Jehovah Rapha, the healer, He will heal. God will answer and be with us even if we encounter trouble.

> With a long life I will satisfy him and I will let him see My salvation.
>
> —PSALM 91:16

Pray for deliverance, welfare, prosperity, and victory. This is the time to declare length of days and fulfillment of purpose.

Eighth watch (3:00 p.m.–6:00 p.m.)

This was the time when Peter and John entered the temple and healed the lame man at the gate (Acts 3:1–10). Pray for healing to be released upon those who have been captive to sickness and disease. Pray that miracles will be released on the earth. Pray that miracles would glorify God and show His compassion toward mankind. God wants to show that He is God alone and many must turn to Him to be saved.

Watch and Pray

> I will stand at my watch and station myself on the watchtower; and I will keep watch to see what He will say to me, and what I will answer when I am reproved.
>
> —HABAKKUK 2:1

If we are going to have results, power, and glory, we must watch and pray. By serving the Lord with prayer day and night, Anna was following the command to keep a continual sacrifice of prayer before the altar. Leviticus 6:12 states that the fire on the altar must never burn out. Habakkuk gives us instruction on how we can keep the watch of the Lord.

+ Stand at your watch. Posture your heart to take a stand, and simply pick a watch from the eight listed above. Don't be religious—pick a time that is convenient for you. With determination, develop your stand and pray with perseverance. The Hebrew for *stand, 'amad*, means "to stand; take one's stand; be in a standing attitude, stand forth, take a stand, present oneself, attend upon, be or become servant of." [11]

+ Station yourself on the watchtower. Be where you can see from God's perspective.

+ Watch to see what God will say to you. Wait on the Lord with an open heart and mind. Check and patrol in the spirit to see if anything needs to be done. Keep a journal of the things the Lord speaks, and pray until they come to pass.

Watchman Prayer

Lord, I pray that You will set me as a watchman on the wall of prayer. Awaken my heart that I may cry out for my generation. Break my heart with the things that break Your heart. Lord, I don't want to be religious; I want to be righteous. You said the effective, fervent prayer of the righteous makes tremendous power available. Let Your grace come upon me to watch and pray. Let me be sensitive to Your leading and prompting. Open my eyes, ears, and heart to perceive Your voice in this hour. Let me be connected to Your Spirit. I want to know the times and seasons of heaven. Let me connect to Your movements on the earth. Give me prophetic insight, discernment, and understanding. I break all prayerlessness off of my life. Your Word says that unless the Lord guards the city, the watchman stays awake in vain. Lord, I want to partner and colabor with you. Set me on the watch You've ordained for me.

Chapter 5

MINISTERING TO THE LORD

And then as a widow to the age of eighty-four. She did not leave the [area of the] temple, but was serving and worshiping night and day with fastings and prayers.

—Luke 2:37, amp

Anna dedicated her entire life to worship, prayer, and fasting. Her lifestyle of consecration speaks volumes to our generation. Serving the Lord or ministering to the Lord is the highest call of any believer. I believe the Lord illuminated a pattern for sustaining a lifestyle of prayer through Anna's life. There will be some women who have a primary calling similar to Anna's, to commit their lives solely to the church, watching, praying, and fasting. Now don't put the book down—I also believe many women will have to cultivate the Anna anointing as a secondary calling, serving as watchmen on a specific prayer watch, because they may also be mothers, wives, and/or working women.

I also believe modern-day women with the Anna anointing will develop the threefold power cord of ministering to the Lord, fasting, and prayer that will release the power of God on the earth. According to Andrew Murray, "We must begin to believe that God, in the mystery of prayer, has entrusted us with a force that can move the heavenly world, and can bring its power down to earth." [1] A right view of God is the foundation of a strong prayer life. "As we pray, we must intentionally take time to recall who He is according to His Word." [2]

The highest calling of any believer is to minister to the Lord. Anna's life paints a beautiful picture of the power of a consecrated life. She separated herself and spent hours blessing His holy name. The modern-day Anna will have a revelation of the significance of developing a priestly ministry. God will always favor women who commit their lives to ministering to Him. Ministering to the Lord includes drawing near to Him, worshipping Him, declaring His worth on the earth, meditating on His Word, and accessing His heart. The modern-day Anna will learn to minister to the Lord before ministering to man. Ministering to the Lord means loving God with all of our hearts.

Created for His Pleasure

> You are worthy, O Lord, to receive glory and honor and power; for You have created all things, and by Your will they exist and were created.
> —Revelation 4:11

God has created us all for His glory. Our hands, feet, and mouths were formed and fashioned to minister to the Lord. We were created for the pleasure of the Lord. The major reason we exist is to bless the Lord. We must endeavor to live lives that glorify Him now and forever. This is a powerful concept to grasp. God gives everyone the power to choose, but we will be held accountable for how we spend our time. The major point here is this: find out what you are called to do, and do it with all your might, remembering it all starts with ministering to the Lord. He created us because He loved us. It was always God's plan to have a royal priesthood and holy nation who would stand before Him to worship His holy name. We were made for God! God loves us and wants to spend time with us. He is a loving Father and loves to hear the human voice in worship and prayer.

Isaiah 43:7 speaks of a people the Lord created for His glory. I believe women with the Anna anointing will have discovered their value in the presence of the Lord. Personally encountering and ministering to the Lord will cause them to obey Him, and understanding His eternal love for them will release confidence and boldness. They will serve and work from a place of love and not for the sake of works or performance. Many times we can develop a works mentality and lose our value and self-worth. As we spend time with the Lord, He will bring breakthrough to our hearts, and we will see ourselves in the light of His glory.

Those with the Anna anointing will understand the significance of ministering to the Lord. It's not burdensome—it is a privilege and honor. It is key to developing your identity; it is key to unlocking your destiny. Worship and prayer are the wisest things we can do. Standing in the presence of the Lord will save your life. I believe the reason Anna wasn't devastated after the death of her husband was because she ministered to the Lord and He ministered to her. She became a living epistle who modeled Psalm 16:11: "You will make known to me the path of life; in Your presence is fullness of joy; at Your right hand there are pleasures for evermore." Anna found her path in life, and so can you. If you're facing confusion regarding who you are and what you're designed to do with your life, try ministering to the Lord. Spend time declaring His name and your love for Him. Remember you are His bride. Just as He did for Anna, He will show you the path of life.

The Language of Worship

You are worthy, O Lord, to receive glory and honor and power; for You have created all things, and by Your will they exist and were created.
—REVELATION 4:11

We can get a picture of how to minister to the Lord from looking at how He is ministered to in heaven. The Lord is worthy "to receive glory." How does God receive glory? It is by the declaration of our lips. We must give Him the glory due His name. A modern-day Anna will express the priestly office by offering the fruit of her lips in praise and worship. A modern-day Anna will extol the Lord and declare His majesty on the earth.

Ministering to the Lord can be expressed through worship. Worshipping is ascribing worth to someone. *Worship* comes from Old English words meaning "[a] condition of being worthy, dignity, glory, distinction, honor, renown; reverence paid to a supernatural or divine being."[3] Based on this definition, we could say that we minister to God by declaring His worth on the earth. We can never truly worship God if we don't understand His worth. There is great value in spending time with the Lord. He becomes our shield and exceedingly great reward. He comes to commune with us.

The modern-day Anna must develop a worship vocabulary. Meditating on the name and nature of the Lord ignites our passion for service. When developing your worship language, it is a good idea to start with Psalm 145 or Revelation 5:12. Below are some words from Psalm 145 (NKJV, emphasis added) that can be used to develop a worship language:

> I will *extol* You, my God, O King; and I will bless Your name forever and ever. Every day I will bless You, and I will praise Your name forever and ever. Great is the LORD, and greatly to be praised; and His *greatness* is unsearchable. One generation shall praise Your works to another, and shall *declare* Your *mighty* acts.... They shall utter the memory of Your great *goodness*, and shall sing of Your *righteousness*. The LORD is gracious and full of compassion, slow to anger and great in mercy. The

LORD is good to all, and His tender mercies are over all His works.... Your saints shall bless You. They shall speak of the *glory* of Your kingdom, and talk of Your power... Your *dominion* endures throughout all generations.... *You open Your hand* and satisfy the desire of every living thing....The LORD is near to all who call upon Him, to all who call upon Him in truth. He will fulfill the desire of those who fear Him; He also will hear their cry and save them.... My mouth shall speak the praise of the LORD, and all flesh shall bless His holy name forever and ever.

+ *Extol* means "to praise highly; to lift up; to elevate; as to extol one's virtues; to elevate by praise." [4] Many times we place God on our level, but we must remember He is above all of our situations and circumstances. We must begin in prayer with the right view of God. The modern-day Anna must resolve in her heart that God is high and powerful.

+ *Greatness* means "the state of being larger in size, quality, or quantity; beyond the ordinary." [5] God's greatness describes "the extent and magnitude of [His] qualities." [6] God is above the ordinary; nothing is impossible with Him. It is important to speak of His greatness to the next generation so the name of the Lord is perpetuated on the earth. This is key to the Anna anointing—as you spend time in the presence of God, beholding the vastness of His greatness, you will feel an unction to declare it to others.

+ *Declare* means "to announce the existence of; to make an unreserved statement" or "to proclaim or avow some opinion or resolution; to make known explicitly some determination."[7] In the place of worship there is boldness and confidence in the existence of God. As you declare the glory, majesty, and power of God, He will manifest Himself in those expressions.

+ *Mighty* means "very powerful in any way, physically, mentally, or morally; having great command; performed with great power." God is supreme; it is He who performs all things. Anna was the first to proclaim Christ. I believe that meditating on His mighty acts will give women with the Anna anointing the faith to perform and proclaim mighty acts of God.

+ *Goodness* means "the state or quality of being good; virtue; excellence; kindness; generosity; benevolence; the best part, essence, or valuable element of a thing."[8] The goodness of God is a fundamental truth. When we enter the presence of the Lord, we must understand and declare His goodness. We must believe that He is good and He will hear and answer prayer. God is the source of all that is good, and His goodness is extended to us.

+ *Righteousness* means "purity of heart and rectitude of life...includes all we call justice, honesty, and virtue, with holy affections."[9] God is righteous; there is no crookedness in Him. He is gracious and full of compassion toward His children. God is righteous in all of His ways and kind in all of His actions. This gives us confidence to pray concerning crooked, rough places in our society. If we're going to rule and reign in this life, we must take up the scepter of righteousness. The modern-day Anna will cultivate a heart of righteousness and pray in the Spirit with authority.

+ *Glory* in the Hebrew means "weightiness; that which is substantial or heavy; glory, honor, splendor, power, wealth, authority, magnificence, fame, dignity, riches, and excellency."[10] I believe that everything we need is found in the glory of God. Isaiah 60:1 states that the glory of the Lord will rise upon believers. The weight of God's glory resting upon our lives is something to be honored and revered. Glory will restore dignity and honor in the church. The glory of God distinguishes true believers from those who practice false religion.

+ *Dominion* means "sovereign or supreme authority; the power of governing and controlling; sovereignty; supremacy."[11] In the place of worship, we must make known to the sons of men the dominion of the kingdom. The modern-day Anna will have a revelation of the supreme power of God's kingdom. Her prayers will extend far beyond her immediate existence to the generations to come.

+ *You open Your hand* speaks of the security, providence, provision, protection, and miracles of God. In the place of worship we see the power of the hand of the Lord. God is always ready to give good things to His children. God upholds all who fall, who are too weak to keep themselves stable. The modern-day Anna will understand the Lord responds to our cry in worship. The Lord will fulfill our petitions and deliver us from the wicked.

God is seeking those who will worship Him in spirit and in truth. As we declare His nature, He is enthroned in our praises.

There are many other words in Revelation and Psalms that can develop your worship vocabulary.

The Diversity of Prayer

> With all prayer and petition pray [with specific requests] at all times [on every occasion and in every season] in the Spirit, and with this in view, stay alert with all perseverance and petition [interceding in prayer] for all God's people.
>
> —Ephesians 6:18, amp

It is important to note that there are different kinds of prayers listed in the Bible. If we're going to see breakthrough and the release of the glory of God, we must be open to flow with the Holy Spirit in diversity. We can ascertain from Ephesians 6:18 that there are many prayers that should be prayed for the saints of God. Intercessory prayer takes on many different expressions, but the motivation is the same: the release of God's kingdom upon the earth.

Prayer of repentance

> *Father, I come boldly to the throne of grace to obtain mercy and find grace in time of need. I ask that You will have mercy on me according to Your lovingkindness and tender mercies. Blot out my transgressions and wash me thoroughly from my sin. Lord, I ask that You create in me a clean heart and renew a righteous spirit within me. I repent of* [fill in what you need to repent of]. *Lord, I ask that You forgive me. I acknowledge my sin, and I ask that You purge me with hyssop and cleanse me from sin. Let joy and gladness return to my heart. In Jesus's name I pray.*

Prayer of worship

Lord, I give You the glory due Your name. All blessing and honor and glory and power be unto You! Lord, You are great and greatly to be praised! Your greatness is unsearchable. There is no one like You. I bless You and magnify Your name. You are great, and You are a miracle worker. Let all creation bow down before You! I declare You are worthy! You are worthy to receive honor. Holy are You, Lord! Faithful are You, Lord! You are merciful, gracious, and slow to anger. Lord, You are good to me, and I love You with my all of my heart and soul and all that I know. My soul makes its boast in You. Be exalted in the heavens. Be magnified on the earth. Power belongs to You, God, and You rule and reign on the earth! Let Your ways be known on the earth and Your salvation among the nations!

Chapter 6

ASK, SEEK, KNOCK

O people in Zion, inhabitants in Jerusalem, you shall weep no more. He will be very gracious to you at the sound of your cry. When He hears it, He will answer you.

—Isaiah 30:19

God hears and answers the prayers of the righteous! This is the hour the Holy Spirit is wooing a generation of women to lift up their voices with bold, audacious prayers. The days of praying "now I lay me down to sleep" prayers are over. The Anna anointing will empower women to embrace new possibilities in the place of prayer.

Many of us have been trained to pray and ask God for things based on what we think we deserve, but those who have cultivated an Anna anointing will ask for things based on His love for them. God is our Father; He loves to give good gifts to His children. So why not ask Him for nations, cities, revival, and spiritual awakening? The possibilities are limitless. God is liberating intercessors from seeing the world from a human perspective. He is enlarging the scope of our perception to view the world from a heavenly perspective. The earth, all its fullness, and those who dwell in it are the Lord's. Our intercession can influence the earth. We don't have to sit idly by and watch disasters happen; we can ask God to intervene. We can pray to have evil rulers replaced, unjust laws reversed, and systemic poverty broken. Those with the Anna anointing will pray for change in every area of life.

This is a critical hour in history. Moral decadence, physical and economic drought, and spiritual decline have left nations impoverished in many ways. Gross darkness is covering the earth. Many have lost hope and believe that the moral depravity of culture is irreversible, but it is not. God promised in Psalm 2:8 that if we ask of Him, He will give us the nations for our inheritance and the ends of the earth for our possession. The destinies of nations are in the hands of intercessors, including women with the Anna anointing.

Ask Anything in My Name

> I will do whatever you ask in My name, that the Father may be glorified in the Son. If you ask anything in My name, I will do it.
>
> —JOHN 14:13–14

God promised that if we ask anything in His Name, He will do it. We need a revelation of the spiritual authority given to us based on our relationship with the Lord Jesus Christ. In His sovereignty and wisdom He has reserved blessings and break-throughs for a generation if His people will only rise up in faith and ask Him. There is authority in asking in the name of Jesus. We must understand the width and scope of the authority that is in the name of Jesus.

Jesus established His authority over the laws of nature by walking on water (Matt. 14:25). He demonstrated the power of the spoken word to control the forces of nature (Mark 4:39). Jesus showed us prayer can alter the laws of physics when He multiplied food and turned water into wine (Matt. 14:19–20; John 2:7–9). Jesus demonstrated authority over disease by healing the multitudes (Matt. 4:23). Jesus displayed the power of crying out when He raised Lazarus from the dead (John 11:43–44). He even defeated the ultimate enemy, death, by being raised from the dead (Rom. 6:9). Then He said, "All authority has been given to Me in heaven and on earth" and gave us this authority (Matt. 28:18; Luke 10:19). He gave us the right and the permission to use His name.

One of the major vehicles for executing the authority of Jesus is prayer. We can rule and reign by exercising the power of the kingdom of God through the scepter of prayer. There is no higher authority than the praying believer seated on heaven's throne with Christ (Eph. 2:6). God will not release blessings, breakthroughs, healing, or revival in our land until the people of the Lord humble themselves, pray, seek His face, and turn from wicked ways. We must awaken to the authority the Lord has given us to affect the quality of life on the earth. God chose the body of Christ to fully express the power Jesus obtained on the cross to the earthly realm.

Shameless Persistence

And He said to them, Which of you who has a friend will go to him at midnight and will say to him, Friend, lend me three loaves [of bread], for a friend of mine who is on a journey has just come, and I have nothing to put before him; and he from within will answer, Do not disturb me; the door is now closed, and my children are with me in bed; I cannot get up and supply you [with anything]? I tell you, although he will not get up and supply him anything because he is his friend, yet because of his *shameless persistence* and insistence he will get up and give him as much as he needs. So I say to you, *Ask* and *keep on asking* and it shall be given you; *seek* and *keep on seeking* and you shall find; *knock* and *keep on knocking* and the door shall be opened to you.

> For everyone who asks and keeps on asking receives;
> and he who seeks and keeps on seeking finds; and to
> him who knocks and keeps on knocking, the door shall
> be opened.
>
> —Luke 11:5–10, ampc, emphasis added

God desires to give good things to His children. He will give us whatever we ask for, yet one of the foundational principles in the kingdom is that we must ask. Everything in the kingdom is voice activated. We must verbalize our need to the Father. Yes, God knows our needs before we ask, but He is interested in developing intimate relationships with His children. He wants to connect with us in the place of asking so we can interact with His heart.

Jesus gives us an exhortation to ask, seek, and knock in prayer. Asking, seeking, and knocking are ascending levels of determination in the realm of prevailing prayer. Asking, seeking, and knocking are continuous actions. This type of prayer is a prayer of importunity. *Importunity* is defined as "shameless persistence." It is making a repeated, annoying request or demand. If we are going to see revival and spiritual awakening, we must have fixed determination to see the goodness of God in the land of the living. Modern-day women with the Anna anointing will be sincere, fervent, constant, persistent, and enduring in seeking the face of God. These women will be insistent in prayer. Those with an Anna anointing will press the needs of this generation before the throne of God "with an energy that never tires, a persistency which will not be denied, and a courage that never fails."[1] This type of prayer increases in intensity. The prayer of importunity is shameless because it has no regard for self. The modern-day Anna will have the heart of importunity with no regard for herself; she will be so caught up with the need of another that she thinks only of the need and how God can fill it. God is releasing an anointing on the modern-day Anna to wait with perseverance and develop courage to never surrender until the grace and glory of the Lord fill the earth.

Asking Prayer

> Ask and it will be given to you.
> —MATTHEW 7:7

The first level of importunate prayer is asking. *Ask* in this scripture can be defined as "[to] beg, call for, crave, desire, or require."[2] This is not casual asking—it is crying out to someone with great authority for intervention. It is a humble acknowledgement of a higher authority as the source of deliverance. This level of prayer has intensity and earnestness that borders on desperation. This type of prayer calls out with a loud and strong cry in order to get someone's attention.

David gave us a perfect example of a crying-out prayer: "Evening and morning and at noon I will pray, and cry aloud, and He shall hear my voice" (Ps. 55:17, NKJV). The Hebrew word for *cry aloud* means "to murmur, growl, roar, cry aloud, mourn, rage, sound, make noise, tumult, be clamorous, be disquieted, be loud, be moved, be troubled, be in an uproar."[3] There is a generation of women who will not be silenced by fear, religion, or indifference. Women will gather in places of prayer to create uproar in the spirit over the complacent, passionless church. There will be a tumultuous sound; they will put terror in the heart of the enemy. The sound will cause the earth to shake and God to rend the heavens and come down in power and glory (Ps. 18:6–9). Those who ask and cry out to God move His hand and heart. He comes with mighty acts upon the earth. These prayer gatherings will resemble those in the Book of Acts—they will shake the very foundations of the earth, setting captives free and bringing healing and deliverance to the bound and revival upon the earth.

Seeking in Prayer

Seek and you will find.

—MATTHEW 7:7

The second level of importunate prayer is seeking. Once you've asked God in prayer, the next step is to seek His face for the answer. This level of prayer goes beyond surface solutions and Band-Aid remedies for life's most difficult challenges. This level of praying starts with the resolve to keep seeking until the required object is found. There is a resolution in the heart of the intercessor to receive the answer to prayer. There is a fixed determination to seek and diligently entreat the mind of God, to search earnestly until the object of the search is located. The Greek word for *seek* in this passage means "to seek in order to find; to seek a thing; to seek [in order to find out] by thinking, meditating, reasoning, to enquire into; to seek after, seek for, aim at, strive after; to seek; i.e., require, demand; to crave, demand something from someone."[4]

Seeking prayer involves seeking the face of the Lord, His presence, and His counsel in a situation. It is inclining the heart, attentively listening with spiritual ears, and searching for understanding. This prayer involves searching the Scriptures, proclaiming the promises of God, and seeking the discernment and wisdom of God. This will require meditating on the Word and spending time in solitude until God comes with the awaited answer. This type of prayer implies the close pursuit of God. You diligently seek God because you know that He alone has the answer to your problem. He has promised that He is a rewarder of those who diligently seek Him (Heb. 11:6).

There are many things happening in our society that require careful investigation and inquiring of the Lord. Many times in prayer we find ourselves at a loss for words and our understanding of the Lord's will is unfruitful, but the Lord promised the Holy Spirit will help us in our weaknesses. The Holy Spirit will teach us to pray as we ought, or as the occasion demands (Rom. 8:26). The Holy Spirit will enlighten the eyes of our understanding as we pray in our spiritual language with tongues in the Spirit.

Knocking Prayer

> Knock and it will be opened to you.
>
> —MATTHEW 7:7

The third realm of importunate prayer is knocking. Doors are opened and shut in the spirit by believers praying and speaking God's words on the earth. Once you have asked God, sought His face, and obtained an answer, there must be a birthing or even a time of travail before the answer is manifested on the earth. This prayer may even require warfare. The Greek word for *knock* means "to strike; to knock [on a door] with a heavy blow."[5] This type of intercession strikes the mark or target in prayer like lightning. Job 36:32 says, "He covers His hands with lightning, and commands it to strike" (NKJV). The Hebrew word for *strike* is the same word used for *intercession*; it means "strike the mark; plead; urge."[6]

Knocking prayer is continual praying, a quest for God's order in God's timing. Have you ever knocked on a door just once? We instinctively knock on a door several times to ensure the knock is heard. Knocking prayer takes hold of the will of God in a situation, bears down, and wrestles until it gives birth to the answer. Knocking in prayer involves groaning and travail. God hears the groans of His people:

> In the passing of time the king of Egypt died. And the children of Israel sighed because of the bondage, and they cried out, and their cry came up to God on

account of the bondage. God heard their groaning, and
God remembered His covenant with Abraham, Isaac,
and Jacob. God looked on the children of Israel, and
God had concern for them.

—EXODUS 2:23–25

Much as it is today, the children of Israel were under extreme
duress, oppression, and bondage. They needed salvation and
deliverance. God heard their groaning and moved to deliver
them. God is awakening the groan once again! There is so much
bondage and despair in the land. A modern-day Anna will weep,
groan, and travail for freedom from bondage, deliverance from
enemy oppression, and life and victory on the earth. Knocking in
prayer is similar to travail in that it results in birth. Those with
an Anna anointing will labor to see revival come to the nations
of the earth. The anointing needed to bring forth the will of God
is compared to childbirth; this anointing is laced with love and
passion for the lost. The Holy Spirit is exposing the Father's
heart through an intensified burden when words are inade-
quate. *Travail* is defined as "physical or mental exertion; agony;
labor [of childbirth]."[7] Knocking in prayer is a "birthing" kind
of prayer. Knocking in prayer opens doors of access in the spirit
realm. Knocking in prayer opens doors that the gospel may be
preached and may advance on the earth. Give yourself completely
to knocking in prayer. Your groans, tears, and weeping will reach
beyond the visible to the throne of God.

Asking, seeking, and knocking in prayer will yield great returns
in the days to come. I want to admonish you to embrace importunate praying and refuse to be denied the greatness the Lord
has promised for you and this generation. Enter the presence of
the Lord with humility and submission, yet with holy boldness,
asking your heavenly Father for what you want. Let tenacity and
perseverance motivate you. Don't be so eager to place a period at

the end of your prayer when God wants to place a comma. Keep asking, keep seeking, and keep knocking until you are in the face of God, until you are assured that something has shifted in your life, until revival comes, until violence is no longer heard in your streets, until your sons and daughters are saved, until you are healed, until the name of Jesus is famous in our land, and until the knowledge of the glory covers the earth!

Prayer for the Nations of the Earth

Father, I ask You for the salvation of the nations of the earth. You said that if we ask, You will give us the nations for our inheritance and the uttermost parts of the earth as our possessions. Lord, save our land. I humble myself. I come to You praying and crying out, for You will heal our land. I turn from my wicked ways. Lord, forgive us for being prideful and hard-hearted. I ask that You will come with revival and spiritual awakening. I ask that You will be merciful to us and bless us with Your presence. Let Your face shine upon us. Lord, we need Your wisdom in our land. I bind every antichrist devil that is loosed in the nations of the earth. Father, bring peace in our nations. Let Jesus, the Prince of Peace, be preached in every nation of the earth. Let the greater-works generation arise, those who will preach the gospel with power and demonstration, those who will not compromise Your standard of righteousness.

Chapter 7

IDENTIFICATION INTERCESSION

Remember the marks of the true intercessor....A sense of the
need of souls; a Christlike love in the heart; a consciousness
of personal impotence; faith in the power of prayer; courage
to persevere in spite of refusal; and the assurance of an abundant reward.[1]

—ANDREW MURRAY

I LOVE THIS quote from Andrew Murray. The mark of a true
intercessor is "a sense of the need of souls." We have lost the concept of being our brother's keeper. We must return to loving our
neighbors as ourselves. Mankind has needs and weaknesses that
only Jesus can help them with. The modern-day Anna will reach
toward Him for mercy and reach toward people and nations
to connect the gap; she will be a go-between to connect heaven
and earth through identification intercession. She will reach to
heaven to release healing and deliverance in the lives of people.

God is beckoning the church to move beyond ordinary prayer.
The days of praying routine prayers and prayer lists are coming
to an end. Those methods served the purpose of jump-starting
our prayer lives. They were the training wheels in the spirit. We
must move beyond praying for our needs and the needs of our
family members. There is a lost and dying world confused by
the power of darkness. The church cannot sit idly by while our
world advances into moral decay and false religion. It is time for a
shift into action. Jesus gave the church her core identity when He

stated, "My house shall be called a house of prayer for all nations" (Mark 11:17). It is time to take up the mantle.

There is another level of prayer needed in this time of human history. The church has become indifferent and callous to the needs of our cities and nations. Forty-two percent of the world's population is a part of an unreached people group.[2] Women with the Anna anointing are being called and chosen by the Spirit of God to abandon the culture of self-absorption, self-gratification, and self-indulgence to embrace identification intercession. Identification intercession identifies with the one whom the intercessor is praying for, pleading his or her cause before the throne of God. This type of intercession puts the needs of others before personal needs. This will require embracing a lifestyle-motivated self-denial, embodying what it truly means to be a disciple of Christ. This type of intercession involves dying to self and giving your life in prayer for others. The intercessor can feel what others feel by the power of the Holy Ghost, resulting in prevailing prayer.

One of the greatest expressions of love is found in the act of identification intercession. "Greater love has no man than this: that a man lay down his life for his friends" (John 15:13). Identification intercession will bring in the greatest harvest of souls. Identification intercession also causes the blessings of the Lord to boomerang onto the life of the intercessor.

Jesus: The Chief Intercessor

In the days of His flesh, Jesus offered up prayers and supplications with loud cries and tears to Him who was able to save Him from death. He was heard because of His godly fear.

—HEBREWS 5:7

Hebrews 7:24–25 states, "But He, because He lives forever, has an everlasting priesthood. Therefore He is able to save to the uttermost those who come to God through Him, because He at all times lives to make intercession for them." Jesus, the King of the universe, is an intercessor. He has all power in His hand yet lives to make intercession for mankind. That's fascinating! Priestly mediation is part of the ongoing ministry of Jesus. Those of us with the Anna anointing get the awesome privilege of connecting with the prayers Jesus is praying right now.

Identification prayer models Jesus's work on the earth. The ultimate expression of intercession was the sins of the entire world being laid upon Jesus. Two thousand years ago Jesus's blood atoned for our sins, and our salvation is secure. Jesus made a way for every human to approach God personally and develop a personal relationship with the heavenly Father. He stood in the gap for mankind by dying on the cross. Jesus was the scapegoat that carried our sins away forever. In order to intercede for us, He first became one with us, identifying with us in our flesh, feeling our infirmities, and being tempted in all things even as we are. (See Hebrews 2:14–17.)

Identification intercession takes hold of the sin in prayer and carries it before the throne of grace to obtain mercy on behalf of the sinner. This type of prayer requires humility and a broken and contrite heart. Intercession is expressed in two ways. The first expression is identifying with sinful men, and secondly, identifying with God.

Examples of Identification Intercession

Interceding for our nations, cities, and families requires humility and brokenness. Many great men and women in Scripture set a powerful example of identification intercession. Our first example is found in the expression of the priestly ministry in the

Old Testament. The priests modeled the work of identification intercession. They had to go before a holy God and present sacrifices for the sin of the land. They stood in the gap and made the hedge between God and man. Let's look at some other examples of identification intercession.

Daniel

> O Lord, according to all Your righteousness, I beseech You, let Your anger and Your fury be turned away from Your city Jerusalem, Your holy mountain, because for our sins and for the iniquities of our fathers, Jerusalem and Your people have become a reproach to all who are around us.
>
> —DANIEL 9:16

Daniel gives us an example of the posture of the intercessor's heart: "because for our sins and for the iniquities of our fathers, Jerusalem and Your people have become a reproach to all who are around us."

He identified with the sin. He was not pointing the finger at another generation; he took ownership of the sin. He reminded God of His character and righteousness. He confessed the sin. He prayed for the entire nation.

Nehemiah

> They said to me, "The remnant that returned from captivity is there in the province enduring great affliction and reproach. Also, the wall of Jerusalem remains broken down, and its gates have been burned with fire." When I heard these words, I sat down and wept and mourned for days. Then I fasted, and prayed before the God of heaven, and said: "I beseech You, O LORD God

of heaven, the great and awesome God, who keeps covenant and mercy for those who love Him and keep His
commandments. Let Your ear now be attentive, and
Your eyes open, that You may hear the prayer of Your
servant, which I now pray before You, day and night,
for the children of Israel Your servants, and confess
the sins of the children of Israel, which we have sinned
against You. Both my father's house and I have sinned."

—NEHEMIAH 1:3–6

Nehemiah was the king's cup bearer. He lived in the luxury
and comfort of the palace. He could have been indifferent to the
plight of his people. But Nehemiah heard of the condition of his
nation, which activated compassion in his heart. This compassion moved him to stand in the gap for his nation. When devastation and destruction come, God will awaken identification
intercession in the hearts of intercessors to petition for His intervention. When you hear evil reports about your city or nation,
don't feel helpless. Open your mouth and cry out in intercession.
Remember, God hears and answers prayers.

Nehemiah began to weep, mourn, and fast because he loved
the people. Love is the greatest motivation for intercession.
Nehemiah had a broken and contrite heart before the Lord.
These are instruments of identification intercession. They are
an expression of godly sorrow. Godly sorrow will bring men to
repentance.

Nehemiah acknowledged the sovereign nature of God, who
acts according to His promises. Nehemiah identified with the
sin of his ancestors. Nehemiah confessed the sin. He used the
Word of God to remind God of His promises and ask for mercy.

God is the same yesterday, today, and forever. What was
effective in the days of Daniel and Nehemiah is effective now.
Daniel and Nehemiah demonstrated the power of identification

intercession to bring revival, reformation, restoration, and reconciliation to a generation. Identification intercession is the mediating and reconciling ministry of the Lord Jesus. Daniel and Nehemiah gave us a pattern to follow for effective identification intercession:

+ Develop a heart of compassion

+ Fast and pray for the nation, city, or people

+ Identify with the sin

+ Acknowledge the sovereignty and righteous nature of God

+ Confess the sin

+ Demonstrate godly sorrow over the sin

+ Use the Word of God to remind God of His promises

+ Ask God for mercy on behalf of the people, nation, or city

Results of Identification Intercession

> God was in Christ reconciling the world to Himself, not counting their sins against them, and has entrusted to us the message of reconciliation. So we are ambassadors for Christ, as though God were pleading through us. We implore you in Christ's stead: Be reconciled to God. God made Him who knew no sin to be sin for us, that we might become the righteousness of God in Him.
> —2 CORINTHIANS 5:19–21

Identification intercession's end result is reconciling man to God. The ministry of reconciliation is the process by which God and man are brought together again. Modern-day women akin to Anna are ambassadors for Christ who plead in prayer for others who may not be ready to encounter the fullness of life in Jesus. Through intercession, women with the Anna anointing release love and deliverance to the needy.

Identification intercession causes the original plans and purposes of God to be restored on the earth. Joel 2 reveals the power of weeping, mourning, and fasting to bring restoration on the earth. *Restore* is defined as "to bring back or put back into a former or original state."[3] In the Bible, when something is restored, it is always increased or improved so that the end state is better than the original state. "God multiplies when He restores."[4] Jesus really wants us to have life and life more abundantly. There must be a company of women with the Anna anointing who will appeal to the merciful heart of God for a spiritual awakening in our generation.

God's Chosen Fast

This is the kind of fast day I'm after: to break the chains of injustice, get rid of exploitation in the workplace, free the oppressed, cancel debts. What I'm interested in seeing you do is: sharing your food with the hungry, inviting the homeless poor into your homes, putting clothes on the shivering ill-clad, being available to your own families. Do this and the lights will turn on, and your lives will turn around at once. Your righteousness will pave your way. The GOD of glory will secure your passage. Then when you pray, GOD will answer. You'll call out for help and I'll say, "Here I am."

—ISAIAH 58:6–8, THE MESSAGE

The two major hindrances to effective identification intercession are indifference and hardness of heart. *Indifference* means "lack of interest or concern." Synonyms include unconcern, listlessness, apathy, and insensibility, all of which imply a lack of feeling.[5] *Hardness of heart* means one's heart is cold, callous, unfeeling, or unyielding.[6] In Scripture *hardness of heart* refers to "a persistent inner refusal to hear and obey the word of God" or "an uncaring or unsympathetic attitude towards other people."[7] Hardness of heart and indifference are rooted in pride. Fasting is a spiritual tool that will help you to develop humility and soften your heart.

God's chosen fast will have you take your eye off of your needs and focus on others. Fasting is abstaining from food. It will tenderize your heart to the plight of mankind. Experiencing hunger can give you compassion for the hungry. Fasting humbles the soul. Fasting causes us to turn from food and turn toward God.

Fasting is a biblical discipline. Below is a list of benefits of fasting from Isaiah 58:

+ Causes your voice to be heard on high

+ Looses the bonds of wickedness

+ Undoes heavy burdens

+ Frees the oppressed

+ Breaks every yoke

+ Gives you a generous spirit

+ Fosters a spirit of hospitality

+ Encourages you to care for your family and extended family

+ Helps you access the spirit of revelation and wisdom; answers to questions

- Breaks the spirit of infirmity; delayed healing springs forth

- Extends a scepter of righteousness to you

- Makes the glory of God your rear guard; protection from God Himself

- Gives you a new connection to the heart of God

- Dullness of hearing is broken; you can quickly discern the voice of the Lord

- Hardness of heart is broken; you can receive the counsel of the Lord

- Spiritual drought is broken; you can experience refreshing from the Lord

- Breaks generational poverty

- Releases generational blessings

- Purifies your heart and your speech

Prayers for Revival and Spiritual Awakening

O Lord, according to all Your righteousness, I beseech You, let Your anger and Your fury be turned away from Your city Jerusalem, Your holy mountain, because for our sins and for the iniquities of our fathers, Jerusalem and Your people have become a reproach to all who are around us....O Lord, hear! O Lord, forgive! O Lord, listen and act! Do not defer, for Your own sake, O my God. For Your city and Your people are called by Your name.

—DANIEL 9:16, 19

Godly sorrow produces repentance that leads to salvation and brings no regret, but the sorrow of the world produces death.

—2 Corinthians 7:10

Father, I ask that You will release the spirit of conviction upon the hearts of men once again. Let there be a deep conviction of sin once again. Many have become politically correct, leaving the truth of the gospel. I pray that leaders will preach the truth of Your Word once again. Let the anointing of the refiner's fire be released in Your church. Purify and burn out anything in our hearts that is not like You. Your Word says that the product of godly sorrow is repentance. Lord, I pray that the body of Christ will come to true repentance, confession, and action. I pray that true spiritual brokenness would return to the church. Let there be a returning to fasting, weeping, and mourning. Let the pastors in my nation preach messages that bring true repentance.

Pray for a fresh commitment to holiness—a commitment to radical holiness and purity, a commitment to abstain from evil, and an understanding of righteousness (Lev. 11:44; 2 Cor. 7:1; Titus 2:12).

Lord, we need a great awakening. Let the holy fear of the Lord return to the church again. Father, cause this generation to return to Your ways. Let holiness and righteousness be honored in the church again. Let there be an increased awareness of Your presence, God, and a new hunger for righteousness. I desire to see Your glory cover the earth like the waters cover the sea. Let Your manifest presence return to the earth. Let revival break

*out in my country. Let the kingdom of God break in
with power. Let miracles, signs, and wonders be released
in my city.*

*I pray for our leaders: let them live lives of holiness
and righteousness; let them be men and women of righteousness; let them carry the true burden of the Lord.
Let the spirit of boldness come upon leaders to speak
Your Word. I break the spirit of fear off of my leader.
Let leaders be fearless and proclaim the gospel as they
ought. I release boldness. I release revelation and insight
from the Holy Ghost.*

*Let the power of the Holy Ghost empower leaders to
preach with signs and wonders following. Let them be
given utterances from heaven to make known the mysteries of the gospel. Let the leaders of this generation
arise to be the ambassadors of Christ.*

**Pray for a new commitment to supplication, intercession, and
prayer for all men. Pray that houses of prayer will arise all
over the world with a genuine spirit of prayer produced by
the Holy Spirit (1 Tim. 2:1).**

*Father, unite my heart to fear Your name. You said in
Your Word that blessed are they who hunger and thirst
for righteousness, for they shall be filled. Give me the
gift of hunger. Empty me of religion and traditions of
men. Break me out of the restraining mold of religion.
Deliver me from dead, dry religion. My soul thirsts for
You in a dry and weary land. I come to the well of Your
Spirit and ask You to give me a drink. Give me living
water. Spring up, O well, within me. Let the fountain of
water spring up into a fountain of everlasting life.*

Holy Spirit, we need You! There is no revival without You! I ask that You will release unified prayer throughout the earth. Let the spirit of grace and supplication ignite human hearts with a passion for the living God. Raise up a generation to cry out day and night like Anna and give You no rest until the knowledge of the glory of the Lord covers the earth as the waters cover the sea. Let a genuine spirit of prayer produced by the Holy Spirit be released upon this generation.

Pray for a new commitment to love. Pray that the church will walk in fervent and unfeigned love of the brethren. Let there be unity and fellowship. Let there be a hatred for strife and division (Ps. 133; Rom. 5:5; Gal. 5:13; Eph. 5:2; 1 Pet. 1:22).

Lord, Your Word says how good and pleasant it is for the brethren to dwell together in unity. I pray that You will pour out the bonding oil of unity. Make us one. Let the church experience Your commanded blessing, life forever more. Break down the wall of separation and division. Let those who spread seeds of discord among the brethren be convicted. Lord, I pray that You will heal Your sons and daughters and make us one. I pray that You will make us one as You and Jesus are one. Let loving each other be our highest goal in ministry. Let us learn to love one another that the world may know You came. Let the spirit of love became so tangible that men can see and feel it in the great congregation. Let us fall in love with You so that we may love one another.

I bind all spirits of competition. I loose unity and cooperation. I bind cruelty and jealousy. I bind the spirit of pride and fear. I loose humility and love.

Father, we understand that we cannot love in our own strength. Holy Spirit, empower us to love one another. Pour out the love of God in our hearts.

Pray for a commitment to evangelism and winning the lost (Matt. 9:37).

Lord of the harvest, we pray that You would send forth laborers into the fields. Give believers Your heart for souls. I pray that honor for the evangelist would return to the church. Lord, we repent for not winning souls. Your Word says he who wins souls is wise. Let the spirit of hardness of heart be broken off of believers. Let the scales be removed from our eyes to see the harvest all around us. Let fear and intimidation be broken off of believers. Let us trust You to give us words to speak. Lead us to those to whom we are called to minister the gospel of salvation. Order our steps in Your Word. Let the preachers and proclaimers return to the church.

Pray for a commitment to revival, restoration, and reformation (Isa. 58:12–13; Ps. 85:6).

Father, we ask for a continuous revival in the land. Let Your presence and Your glory cover the earth as the waters cover the sea. Lord, we ask that You restore Your power in the church. Let miracles, signs, and wonders be released. Let the power of the Lord be present to heal. Heal families, relationships, and broken hearts. Let revival start in the heart of every believer. Let there be new commitment to see reformation in the church. Let new churches be planted. Let new ministries be birthed to meet the needs of this generation.

Pray for a new commitment to humility (2 Chron. 7:14).

Father, we humble ourselves under Your mighty hand. We repent of pride, arrogance, vainglory, and haughtiness. We turn from our wicked ways and turn to You. We seek Your face for wisdom and instruction. We ask You to heal our land. Heal our culture. Deliver us from racism and hatred. Let the spirit of forgiveness and reconciliation fill our hearts. Let Your peace return to our nation. In Jesus's name we pray. Amen.

Chapter 8

DEVELOPING THE SPIRIT OF GRACE AND SUPPLICATION

May God open our eyes to see what the holy ministry of intercession is to which, as His royal priesthood, we have been set apart. May He give us a large and strong heart to believe what mighty influence our prayers can exert. And may all fear as to our being able to fulfill our vocation vanish as we see Jesus, living ever to pray, living in us to pray, and standing surety for our prayer-life.[1]

—ANDREW MURRAY

THERE IS POWER and purpose in a name. Every name in the Bible has meaning. Names in the Bible were landmarks and announcements to times and seasons. When the ark of the Lord was captured, the wife of Phinehas gave birth to a child named Ichabod (meaning "no glory"[2]), marking the beginning of a season in Israel's history when the glory had departed. When Jacob wrestled with an angel all night until his nature was changed, he went from being called Jacob, "supplanter,"[3] to Israel, "prince of God."[4]

When we look at the etymology of Anna's name, we can gain great insight into the anointing on her life. We have already pointed out that her name means "grace." Her name comes from a root word meaning "to grant a favor, to be gracious, and to favor."[5] The word "depicts a heartfelt response by someone who has something to give to one who has a need."[6] While the word is used for the actions of people toward people, it is mainly used for the actions of God toward people. A derivation of the word is in the familiar phrase "finding favor." While *Anna* means "grace or favor," it can also mean "ah, now!" or "we beseech thee!"[7] The word *beseech* paints the picture of a person earnestly praying. It means "to beg for urgently or anxiously; to request earnestly; to make supplication."[8] Thus, Anna's name speaks of both grace and supplication.

The modern-day Anna will find favor in the presence of the Lord. She will have favor with God and favor with men. Built into the DNA of those with an Anna anointing is an ability to beseech the Lord with fervency and zeal of intercession. Because they have spent time abiding in the presence of the Lord, they will ask what they will and it shall be given. Those with an Anna anointing will sincerely offer compassionate intercession that moves the heart and hand of God. They will have grace to beseech the Lord to release His mercy and kindness. They will be empowered by the spirit of grace and supplication.

The Spirit of Grace and Supplication

> And I will pour on the house of David and on the inhabitants of Jerusalem the Spirit of grace and supplication; then they will look on Me whom they pierced. Yes, they will mourn for Him as one mourns for his only son, and grieve for Him as one grieves for a firstborn.
>
> —Zechariah 12:10, nkjv

When God is ready to release revival and spiritual awakening in the church, He pours out the spirit of grace and supplication, releasing conviction and repentance. The spirit of grace and supplication will cause you to cry out for Jesus to come to the earth in power and glory. The Holy Spirit is the spirit of grace and supplication that breaks through hardness of heart by causing the heart to be drawn back to Jesus, the Messiah. The modern-day Anna will be anointed by the Holy Spirit with the spirit of grace and supplication to birth new things into earth through long hours of prayer. The Holy Spirit will anoint intercession with a grace that causes a supernatural release of God's ability in us to pray. We cannot pray in our own strength. We need the help of the Holy Spirit. The Holy Spirit is our empowering force as we make supplications before God. Effective prayer is not by might nor by power but by the Spirit.

The Spirit of Grace

> Not by might nor by power, but by My Spirit, says the LORD of Hosts. Who are you, O great mountain? Before Zerubbabel you will be made level ground, and he will bring out the top stone amidst shouting of "Grace! Grace to the stone!"
>
> —ZECHARIAH 4:6–7

Intercessory prayer must be empowered by the grace of God. The Hebrew word for *grace* means "to act graciously or mercifully toward someone; to be compassionate, and to be favorably inclined."[9] The Greek word for *grace* signifies "undeserved favor; a free gift." It is also "the manifestation of God's power exceeding what we could achieve or hope for by our own [labor]."[10] The spirit of grace is divine enablement or empowerment to achieve effective prayer.

One of the major pitfalls of intercessors is to labor in prayer by the might of the flesh and not by the spirit of grace. Ephesians 3:16 gives us the key to Spirit-empowered intercession: "that He would give you, according to the riches of His glory, power to be strengthened by His Spirit in the inner man." It is the Holy Spirit who causes you to be strengthened with an infusion of might in the inner man. The task of prayer will not be accomplished by might or physical stamina; it will only be accomplished through the empowering of the Holy Spirit. Zechariah 4:6–7 shows us the benefit of the spirit of grace: it empowers you to speak to mountains, which represent difficult places and hard situations. Grace-empowered prayers can cause mountains to crumble and fall. The spirit of grace causes your prayers to be filled with compassion for the needy. The spirit of grace will equip you with spiritual stamina and longevity in the place of prayer. I believe it was the spirit of grace that allowed Anna to spend sixty years in the temple.

The Spirit of Supplication and Intercession

> Therefore I exhort first of all that you make supplications, prayers, intercessions, and thanksgivings for everyone.
>
> —1 Timothy 2:1

Luke 2:37 states that Anna served God with fasting and prayer night and day. The Greek word for *prayer* in the passage is the same word used for *supplication*. The spirit of supplication results in steadfast, continuous, unceasing, relentless praying. It is entreating God on behalf of man. The spirit of supplication involves tireless pursuit of God. It is the ability to implore God's aid in a particular matter. It is a specific request. It is a prayer of perseverance and earnest petition. "Be anxious for nothing, but in everything, by prayer and supplication with gratitude, make your requests known to God" (Phil. 4:6). Supplication is the heart conversing with and petitioning God, seeking and asking on behalf of mankind. When the spirit of supplication comes upon you in prayer, you will entreat of the Lord for a specific need in an intense, deep, relentless manner.

The Work of the Holy Spirit

> Likewise, the Spirit helps us in our weaknesses, for we do not know what to pray for as we ought, but the Spirit Himself intercedes for us with groanings too deep for words. He who searches the hearts knows what the mind of the Spirit is, because He intercedes for the saints according to the will of God. We know that all things work together for good to those who love God, to those who are called according to His purpose.
> —ROMANS 8:26–28

The Holy Spirit is God on the earth. He is not wind, fire, or a dove. He can manifest Himself as those things, but He is the Spirit of God that lives inside us. Just let that sink into your heart and mind. We have God living inside of us! The same Spirit that raised Christ from the dead lives inside of you. You have resurrection power living inside of you! This power can be accessed and applied to every situation in your life by prayer and intercession.

Jesus said that He would send the Helper to teach us things. The major area in which the help of the Holy Spirit is experienced is intercession. Whatever you're facing, whether it is confusion, a child on drugs, difficulties in your marriage, or violence in your city, the solution can be found within you. When you connect to the divine power of the Holy Spirit in prayer and intercession, circumstances change.

The apostle Paul gave us a clear picture of the supernatural intercessory ministry of the Holy Spirit. I want to focus on several words and phrases from Romans 8:26–28 in the Greek that provide insight into the work of the Holy Spirit in intercession:

+ *helps*—to take hold with at the side for assistance; to take a share in, help in bearing, to help in general; to take hold with another who is laboring[11]

+ *weaknesses*—"of the soul: want of strength and capacity requisite; to understand a thing; to do things great and glorious; to restrain corrupt desires; to bear trials and troubles"[12]

+ *we ought*—"necessity in reference to what is required to attain some end; a necessity of law and command, of duty, equity; necessity established by the counsel and decree of God, especially by that purpose of his which relates to the salvation of men by the intervention of Christ and which is disclosed in the Old Testament prophecies"[13]

+ *intercedes*—a picture of the Holy Spirit swinging into action to rescue and deliver someone who is in trouble; conveys the idea of a rescue operation[14]

+ *groanings*—sighs, cries[15]

+ *too deep for words*—"not to be uttered, not expressed in words"[16]; words that go beyond natural language to the language of the Holy Spirit

+ *searches*—seeks, investigates, examines[17]

+ *mind*—thoughts, purposes, and deep laid plans[18]

Using the Greek words, let's bring this all together so we can see the comprehensive scope of the work of the Holy Spirit in the prayer. The Holy Spirit helps our weakness in prayer. There are times when we feel overwhelmed and backed into a corner. Global crises, economic failures, and our own mistakes can paralyze us with fear. The Holy Spirit is the comforter and will make intercession for us. There are many plans and purposes for your life that you cannot know in your natural understanding, but the Holy Spirit will reveal the plans God has put in your spirit. According to the will of God, the Holy Spirit makes intercession, or prays perfect prayers, for us. The Holy Spirit investigates the eternal plans of God for your life, city, or nation and reveals them to your human spirit, teaching you to pray as you ought. The Holy Spirit takes hold with us in prayer. He comes alongside us to help devise the right course of action in prayer.

Praying in Our Heavenly Language

> When suddenly there came a sound from heaven like the rushing of a violent tempest blast, and it filled the whole house in which they were sitting. And there appeared to them tongues resembling fire, which were separated and distributed and which settled on each one of them. And they were all filled (diffused throughout their souls) with the Holy Spirit and began to speak in other (different, foreign) languages (tongues), as the Spirit kept giving them clear and loud expression [in each tongue in appropriate words].
>
> —ACTS 2:2–4, AMPC

The outpouring of the Holy Spirit changed everything for the first-century church. The outpouring and infilling opened a world of power and authority to every believer. What occurred on the Day of Pentecost turned ordinary men into extraordinary men. Suddenly a new language was imparted and the power of the Holy Spirit diffused throughout their souls. Tongues of fire and clear and loud expressions of God were given to them super-naturally by the Spirit of God. God is the same yesterday, today, and forever! The outpouring of the Holy Spirit gives everyone the ability to experience the power of God on a personal level. We can receive the infilling of the Spirit to pray in our heavenly language today.

Praying in the spirit is done in a language that is given by the Holy Spirit, not learned. We speak in tongues by the power of the Holy Spirit. Speaking in tongues is speaking in a language that has tones and sounds, each with a different meaning in the spiritual world. Speaking in tongues is evidence of the infilling of the Spirit. It is also used for self-edification (Jude 20). Speaking in tongues is the way the Holy Spirit intercedes through us in prayer.

In order for our prayers to be effective, we need the help of the Holy Spirit. The Holy Spirit causes our prayer lives to become spiritually empowered with fire and passion. The Holy Spirit allows us to pray beyond our human reasoning and limitations. What is the conclusion, then? "I will pray with the spirit, and I will pray with the understanding" (1 Cor. 14:15). The Holy Spirit empowers those with the Anna anointing to pray effective, fervent prayers of grace and supplication.

Prayer for Impartation of the Spirit of Grace and Supplication

Father, I ask that You pour out the spirit of grace and supplication upon my life. Let me pray effective, fervent prayers. Holy Spirit, help me to intercede unceasingly for the lost. Let the grace of God fill my life. Help me to pray Your heart and mind for cities and nations. Infuse my prayers with grace. Restore the spirit of supplication to Your church. Holy Spirit, teach us how to pray prayers of supplication and intercession that we may live godly and peaceable lives in all godliness and reverence upon the earth. Father, I ask You to activate and release a similar grace upon a whole generation of women. Let us pray until the knowledge of the glory of the Lord covers the earth.

Chapter 9

THE WORSHIPPING WARRIOR

Be strong in the Lord and in the power of His might. Put on the whole armor of God that you may be able to stand against the schemes of the devil.

—Ephesians 6:10–11

MODERN-DAY WOMEN AKIN to Anna are worshipping warriors on the earth. The fuel that ignites our warfare is love. Authority comes from revelation of the person and power of Jesus through beholding Him in worship. Women with the Anna anointing will fight and pray without compromise because they have encountered the Holy Warrior. Anna spent countless hours in the presence of the Lord, praying and fasting. Her heart was on fire and connected to the Lord. Ministering to the Lord empowered her to pray with boldness and without compromise. Prayer is a spiritual force by which we fellowship with God and invite His presence and power into our lives. Prayer is the vehicle to invite God's divine intervention into the affairs of men. Prayer is God's appointed means to obtain what we need.

Worshipping Warriors, Arise!

The church has been lulled to sleep and in many cases is oblivious to the battle raging against its very existence. But we must awaken and return to the core identity of the church as stated by Jesus in Mark 11:17: "My house shall be called a house of prayer for all nations." It is time to put on the whole armor of God and embrace the mantle of intercession to stand in the gap for the souls of our nations.

There is an unseen battle raging against Christians. We cannot see it with our natural eyes, yet at times we can feel its effect. The enemy is walking around as a roaring lion seeking to destroy. He wants to kill your dreams and destroy your destiny. God is raising mighty ones to go into battle. Women must be armed, ready, and engaged in the battle for their marriages, their children, and the nations of the earth. It is time to put on our spiritual armor and take a stand against the enemy. God has promised that no weapon formed against us shall prosper (Isa. 54:17). Problems may arise, but they will not prosper if we learn to pray effective prayers against them. Paul admonishes us to put on the whole armor of God in order to withstand the evil forces of hell (Eph. 6:11). The armor is to be used to protect the prayer warrior. The metaphorical use of the armor and battle dress of the first-century Roman soldier points to the fact that we should be engaged in an active battle now! The armor represents spiritual qualities we must implement in our lives to be effective in warfare prayer.

Be Strong in the Lord

Be strong in the Lord and in the power of His might.
—EPHESIANS 6:10, NKJV

Many would argue that since Jesus died on the cross, everything is already finished and the devil is defeated. While the devil has ultimately been defeated, he still seeks to kill, steal, and destroy. God has given us the responsibility to enforce the finished work of the Cross. Just because we are saved does not mean we are immune to the attacks of the enemy. We must be infused with the strength of the Lord to overcome the assault of the enemy.

We have priority access to the power of the Father to reverse every wicked plan, plot, and scheme against our lives. Do not fight in your own strength. "The weapons of our warfare are not carnal, but mighty through God to the pulling down of strongholds" (2 Cor. 10:4).

We must understand that when we pray and intercede, we are partnering with the Spirit of God to bring His will on the earth. Lift your hands right now and receive an impartation of God's strength. You must receive the power and strength of God before you fight in an unseen battle. God will empower us with His strength, for battles are won by the Spirit of the Lord. Being strong in the Lord will keep you from weariness and battle fatigue.

Put On the Whole Armor of God

> Put on the whole armor of God, that you may be able to stand against the wiles of the devil.
>
> —Ephesians 6:11, NKJV

Have you ever been invited to an event and the host forgot to tell you that there was a dress code? Or have you ever attended an event and decided to ignore the dress code? This action usually leaves you feeling vulnerable and out of place, and depending on the host, you may be denied access or entry. Paul gives the key to entering into effective warfare prayer: you must be dressed properly. Putting on the whole armor of God requires intentionality. Putting on the armor assures you of victory in the spirit. Just as you have to go to the closet and select clothing to wear for the day, you should put on the armor of God every day. You must not take any shortcuts when putting on the armor. Every piece must be worn to provide protection and strength. There is a synergy of strength and power released to the fully armed soldier. Putting on the armor of God requires making a decision daily to live as a soldier in the army of the Lord.

The Struggle Is Real

> For we do not wrestle against flesh and blood, but against principalities, against powers, against the rulers of the darkness of this age, against spiritual hosts of wickedness in the heavenly places.
>
> —EPHESIANS 6:12, NKJV

Many have taken a "don't ask, don't tell" approach to the reality of the devil and his kingdom of darkness. Many have resolved to not bother him if he isn't bothering them. But if you ignore the devil, he doesn't go away. The devil is real. His attacks are real. This is not a myth or an old wives' tale. He hates the human race because we were made in the image of God. The Greek word for *wrestle* refers to hand-to-hand conflict, "a contest between two...which is decided when the victor is able to hold his opponent down with his hand upon his neck."[1] Paul is clear that our enemy is not physical but spiritual. We do not want to develop a preoccupation with the devil, but we must not ignore his existence. God will teach your hands to fight and your fingers to war. We must stand against and resist the devil.

Resist and Withstand

> Therefore take up the whole armor of God, that you may be able to withstand in the evil day, and having done all, to stand.
>
> —EPHESIANS 6:13, NKJV

James 4:7 tells us to submit to God and resist the devil so he will flee. The key to being successful in spiritual warfare is to submit to God. You must stand under God's command and submit to His authority before becoming a woman of authority. *Resist* means "to fight against (something); to try to stop or prevent (something); to remain strong against the force or effect of (something)."[2] In the Greek, *withstand* suggests "vigorously opposing, bravely resisting, standing face-to-face against an adversary, standing your ground.... [It] tells us that with the authority and spiritual weapons granted to us we can withstand evil forces."[3] As a woman with the Anna anointing, you are called to resist and withstand.

The Loin Belt of Truth

Stand therefore, having girded your waist with truth.
—Ephesians 6:14, nkjv

A major piece of the Roman soldier's armor was the loin belt. It was the piece that held everything together. The truth of God's Word is what holds everything together for the spiritual warrior. We must continue to study biblical truth, because the enemy's strength is keeping us in ignorance. Many Christians are defeated and destroyed because of lack of knowledge.

The Greek word for *truth* refers to "the attitude of truthfulness."[4] It means "truth as a personal excellence; that [candor] of mind which is free from affectation [pretense], simulation, falsehood, deceit."[5] It not enough to have head knowledge of the truth; we must live the truth. Paul is implying that we must not only become knowledgeable of spiritual truths but also cultivate the attitude of truthfulness. To be girded with truth is to have a mind-set of preparedness and commitment. It is the state of being of a genuine believer who forsakes hypocrisy. Heavenly truth will always defeat an earthly fact. For example, the earthly fact may be that your son needs to be healed from a disease, but the heavenly truth is that by the stripes of Jesus Christ he was healed; so based upon this truth, pray relentlessly until you see the manifestation of healing in his body.

The Breastplate of Righteousness

Having put on the breastplate of righteousness.
—EPHESIANS 6:14, NKJV

This was the piece of armor that defended the heart and the vital organs from attack. Righteousness is the scepter of the kingdom. We have positional righteousness and are being made righteous. Righteousness is a gift from God. When you are praying, many times the enemy will attack your right to oppose him. He will fill your heart with feelings of unworthiness and fear. He will attack with accusations of past failures to paralyze and neutralize your prayers. We can reign in this life by the righteousness of the Jesus Christ.

Shoes of Peace

Having shod your feet with the preparation of the gospel of peace.
—EPHESIANS 6:15, NKJV

The soldier's shoes were uniquely designed to kill. The shoes were made out of leather with spikes on the bottom. This served a twofold purpose: to provide stability in battle and to kill an opponent after they were under the foot. The peace of God surpasses the natural mind or thinking. Jesus, the Prince of Peace, brings blessings, deliverance, and salvation in every area of our lives. We can enter the battle knowing that Christ already won the victory. The peace of God will cause you to walk through difficult places and press through for victory. Peace is important in warfare—it guards your heart from destruction and fear. Peace will cause you to prevail in prayer in the midst of crisis. Peace stands guard around your heart.

The Shield of Faith

> Above all, taking the shield of faith with which you will
> be able to quench all the fiery darts of the wicked one.
> —Ephesians 6:16, nkjv

The shield of the Roman soldier was door-shaped and covered with leather hide. It had to be lubricated with oil every day so the arrows of the enemy would slide off. Faith must be applied every day. Faith comes from hearing and applying the Word of God. Our prayers must be Word-based, Word-focused. Faith is developed as we pray the Word of God. Using your faith will release the explosive power of God and protect you from the enemy.

The Helmet of Salvation

> Take the helmet of salvation.
> —Ephesians 6:17, nkjv

The enemy's primary place of the attack is the mind. He is a master of mind games. Paul told us to cast down imaginations and arguments that exalt themselves against the knowledge of God. Going into prayer without your helmet of salvation will surely get your head cut off by the enemy. The helmet of salvation also protects us from insecurity in our salvation and the strongholds of the enemy. Strongholds are collective ideas that war against the truth of God. Strongholds are rooted in lies. There are three levels of strongholds: personal, cultural, and cosmic. Personal strongholds are of the mind. Cultural strongholds involve agreement with Satan's values in our society; there are many ways that we agree with him and keep those evil values entrenched. Cosmic strongholds in the atmosphere are demonic angels or demonic hosts.

The Sword of the Spirit

And the sword of the Spirit, which is the Word of God.
—EPHESIANS 6:17, NKJV

The Word of God is referred to in two different ways. The *Logos* Word is the written Word, and the *rhema* word is the quickened word of God. The sword of the Spirit is the quickened word of God that is used for the particular situation you are praying about. The Holy Spirit will drop a word in your heart from the written Word with divine knowing, faith, assurance, and confidence to pray. The Word of God must be stored in our hearts. The Holy Spirit will reach down in our reservoir for a scripture that will become a sword we can use to stab the enemy.

Prayer of the Worshipping Warrior

The modern-day Anna must be a worshipping warrior. She needs to be strong in the Lord, to put on the full armor of God, and to go into battle on her knees to defeat the enemy.

> *Lord, make me a warrior. Teach my hands to fight and my fingers to war. I make a decision to put on the whole armor of God that I may stand against every wile, trick, or trap of the devil. I securely fasten my heart and mind*

with the belt of truth. I am a champion of truth. I will live in the truth of Your Word. The truth of Your Word will protect me from all deception and seduction. I cover my heart with the breastplate of righteousness, protecting me from all temptation I may face in the world. I am a preacher of righteousness, proclaiming Your truth to the world. Your righteousness and justice are the foundations of Your throne. I pray that You will let justice roll like a river in the earth. I put on my shoes of peace that I will be a peacemaker wherever I go. I have peace because You are the Prince of Peace. I will not be fearful or anxious. I choose to trust You. I take up the shield of faith to quench every dart of the enemy. I rebuke all doubt and deception. I will be bold and strong in the Lord and the power of His might. I love what God loves and hate what He hates. I fight with Him, advancing His kingdom on the earth. I put on the helmet of salvation to protect my mind. I will live in the power of my salvation. I take up the sword of the Spirit, which is the daily Word of God for my life.

Chapter 10

GOD'S MINISTER OF FIRE

Coming at that moment she gave thanks to the Lord and spoke of Him to all those who looked for the redemption of Jerusalem.

—LUKE 2:38

ANNA ACTUALLY ENCOUNTERED the Messiah, and because of this she was overwhelmed with the desire to tell everyone looking for redemption about His arrival. Women who encounter Jesus are the greatest preachers and revivalists. Modern-day women with the Anna anointing will spend time with God face-to-face, gazing on His splendor, experiencing His glorious presence, and hearing His heartbeat through prayer. Those with the Anna anointing will share the reality of Jesus's love with fiery passion and zeal. They will be glory carriers, women who are baptized with the Holy Ghost and fire. They will preach the gospel with signs and wonders following.

These women will have a unique anointing because they have spent countless hours with the refiner's fire. Passion, purity, and power will exude from their being. "And I will be like a wall of fire all around her, says the LORD, and I will be as glory in her midst" (Zech. 2:5). God's presence will be with them in a tangible way, and His fire will be released through them. They will be preachers of righteousness, motivated by love and demonstrating the love of God to mankind. These women will bring deliverance and healing to those who have been ensnared by the powers of darkness.

The modern-day Anna will love the world and not condemn the world (John 3:16–17). There is a generation that is looking for redemption, and God is raising up an answer to their pain. The Lord is endowing women with miraculous power to influence human hearts for the glory of God. He releases miracles to show that He is a loving God who acts on our behalf. Supernatural healing shows God's compassion, causing many to turn to Him. In Luke 7:16, when Jesus raised the widow's son from the dead, the people said, "God has come to help his people" (NIV).

The power of the Holy Spirit comes to encourage belief in the one true God and validate the message of the messenger. First Thessalonians 1:5–6 says, "For our gospel did not come to you in word only, but also in power, and in the Holy Spirit, and in much assurance, just as you know what kind of men we were among you for your sake. You became followers of us and the Lord, having received the word in much affliction, with joy of the Holy Spirit." There are many who may never agree with women being preachers, but they won't be able to deny the hand of the Lord resting upon our lives. God's hand will empower us to accomplish great healings and deliverance on His behalf.

The Fiery Love of Jesus

> Set me as a seal upon your heart, as a seal upon your arm; for love is strong as death, passion fierce as the grave. Its fires of desire are as ardent flames, a most intense flame. Many waters cannot quench love, neither can floods drown it.
>
> —SONG OF SONGS 8:6–7

Jesus is the only solution for women today. Jesus is the hope for all mankind. Jesus and His love are the motivating force behind everything we do and say. Jesus is our safe place. His love will heal your heart. His love will protect you. The enemy has sent the spirit of fatherly rejection against women, but the Lord is releasing His fiery love to purge and utterly destroy this enemy.

Now is the time to set Jesus's love as a seal upon our hearts. He is our conquering King; His seal of love authorizes our call. In ancient times a king would put a wax seal on an important document that was then stamped with the king's signet ring. These documents were both protected and authenticated by the king's seal, which denoted the king's authority and ownership.[1] Modern-day women akin to Anna will have the seal of the King of kings upon their lives and ministries. God's love will protect them and make all the resources of heaven available to advance the agenda of the kingdom. God's love has to be enough for us. We cannot look for the approval of men or society. We must live to love and please Him! We have been sealed with the Holy Spirit of promise (Eph. 1:13).

God's seal is a seal of fire. His supernatural love will melt the hardest of hearts. The seal of fire will break the spirit of cold love on the earth. Jesus said the love of many will grow cold (Matt. 24:12), but God is placing the fiery seal of His love on women with the Anna anointing. He is making them flames of love that spread throughout the earth.

> [Jesus] will baptize you with the Holy Spirit and with fire.
> —LUKE 3:16

Women with the Anna anointing will be effective preachers of the gospel of the kingdom because they carry the spirit of conviction that leads to repentance. Women are arising as messengers of the Lord. They will move in grace and mercy to proclaim what people need to hear and not what they want to hear. Their hearts are set on fire for God, so their flames affect the world. They will have tongues of fire, causing them to boldly declare the wonders of the Lord without fear of man, and those who look for redemption will be saved. Modern-day women akin to Anna will have spent countless hours gazing in the eyes of Jesus's flaming love. They will be living flames of love that demonstrate the nature of God's all-consuming fire. This fiery love is empowered by an eternal flame from heaven. It is the purified flame taken from the altar of heaven. Satan, the enemy of our souls, "will send the waters of temptation, apathy, disappointment, pain, etc., to put this fire out. [But] God's love poured in our hearts (when continually yielded to) is more powerful than the dark floods of sin and temptation."[2]

In this season God is pouring out His unshakable love, which will enable us to love all people. We are getting ready to experience a surge of revival, and this will cause an influx of people in our lives whom we may have never come in contact with otherwise. We must let God define what love looks like. We must set our affections on things above (Col. 3:2). The Holy Spirit will teach us how to love God and how to love one another. We must love God with all of our minds, hearts, and strength.

We must come to a place of affection-based obedience. Jesus said, "If you love Me, keep My commandments" (John 14:15). This love will cause us to be ready to lay down our lives for others. True love will break through anything and cause us to see the humanity in those who have been dehumanized—even those whom we would normally fear or shy away from. You have the greatest level of influence on people when they know you love them. They will trust you to speak into their lives. They will trust you to pray for them. They will trust you with their lives. Think about it. When you know that God loves you, you can have faith. The Bible says faith works through love (Gal. 5:6). When I know God loves me, I believe what He says even more. When you understand how much He loves you and that He will move heaven and earth on your behalf, you will have faith. This is the love that we are designed to display in order to be an influence to those around us, a love that will spread like fire.

Anna the Prophetic Evangelist

In order to be effective in winning a harvest, a believer must learn to operate in the gifts or manifestation of the Holy Ghost. The world cannot be evangelized without the power and anointing of the Holy Spirit. Jesus heard and saw in the spirit realm by the revelation gifts before He moved in the vocal and power gifts. Jesus was fully God and fully man. He ministered as the last Adam, as a man anointed by the Holy Spirit. He operated through the anointing of the Holy Spirit as believers do today. A modern-day Anna will be equipped with the gifts of the Spirit to bring an effective witness for the Lord. For a greater understanding of the gifts of the Spirit, see my book *The Prophetic Advantage*.

Anna was a prophetess who ministered to those who looked for salvation. She is a prototype for prophets and prophetic believers today. She used her prophetic gift to minister the heart and mind of the Father to a generation. She was a prophetic evangelist. To be prophetic means to declare the counsel of God. It means to know the heart and mind of God for a specific situation. It is the current word proceeding out of the mouth of God. Matthew 4:4 says, "Man shall not live by bread alone, but by every word that proceeds out of the mouth of God." I believe Anna could discern through her prophetic gift which individuals were open to hearing about the Messiah and receiving salvation.

The greatest key to being prophetic is your relationship to the Lord. You will become what you behold. Second Corinthians 3:18 says, "But we all, seeing the glory of the Lord with unveiled faces, as in a mirror, are being transformed into the same image from glory to glory by the Spirit of the Lord." Anna spent her life beholding the face of God. It is safe to say that she knew His heartbeat for her generation. She was sent to the world from the presence of the Lord. She was effective in evangelism because she was empowered with love and prophetic insight.

Let the Lioness Roar!

The Bible uses the lioness as a metaphorical symbol for women. The Lord is causing women to find their voices, and their whispers are transforming into roars against the injustice on the earth. Women will roar with prayer against injustice. Women will roar with preaching against sin and rebellion. Women will roar with prophecy against idolatry. Women will roar against the enemies of God. The lion is known as bold, fearless, powerful, valiant, and strong. Every lion was trained by a lioness. There is a roar coming out of the church, and it is feminine and powerful.

> The lion has roared; who will not fear? The Lord GOD has spoken, who can but prophesy?
>
> —AMOS 3:8

God is calling women to exercise new levels of boldness, courage, and strength. Women must rise up in strength with the Word of the Lord. Lions must roar. A lion without a roar is not much of a lion.

There is a roar coming out of the church through proclamations, decrees, worship, and intercession that will prepare the way for the greatest awakening the world has ever seen. The modern-day Anna will not be able to refrain from declaring what the Lord is saying. There is a stirring in the land. Prophetic women cannot be silent.

Women must be courageous. There is no place for fear and intimidation. We must confront Jezebel and the demons that seek to intimidate and destroy the next generation. The Holy Spirit is anointing women with holy boldness (Acts 4:29).

> The righteous are bold as a lion.
>
> —PROVERBS 28:1

Boldness is related to speech (Acts 19:8). Those who are bold will speak boldly. They will not shut their mouths in fear when they should be speaking. Prophetic women who speak boldly will shatter the powers of darkness with their prophetic declarations. In the Greek, *boldness* means "freedom in speaking, unreservedness in speech; openly, frankly, i.e. without concealment; without ambiguity or circumlocution; free and fearless confidence, cheerful courage, boldness, assurance."[3] One spoken word from the lion-like believer under a prophetic mantle crushes every opposing force. "How forceful are right words!" (Job 6:25). Boldness is the divine enablement of ordinary people to exhibit power and authority.

> The LORD roars from Zion and utters His voice from Jerusalem.
>
> —AMOS 1:2

It is the nature of the lion to roar. The lion's strength and power is manifested through his roar. The Lion of Judah lives inside of you. When God's daughters boldly speak the word God has given them, it is the Lion's roar.

God has a strategic plan for revival and reformation in which women will play a vital role. We are living in a time when God is calling and working through women to fulfill His redemptive plans for mankind. Some will be on the frontlines of society, while others will live consecrated lives of prayer, as did Anna, as their primary assignment. Living a consecrated life before the presence of God is a viable calling from God. God is empowering and equipping women with resolve and determination to find their calling and assignment in the Great Commission. God is calling ordinary women to His extraordinary work. Women will be a sign and wonder to this generation of the greatness and redeeming love of God. The Holy Spirit will empower women to do exploits and fulfill His purposes. Each woman's assignment is unique, but one aspect is always the same: she is on a mission with God to destroy the works of the devil in this generation.

The battle lines are being drawn, and there is a roar coming out of Zion that is feminine, strong, and full of compassion. This roar is from women anointed to preach the gospel of the kingdom, prophesy the word of the Lord, and pray prayers that touch heaven and change earth. God is extending a great invitation to women to serve the purposes of the Lord. These women are overcomers.

The Lord is stirring the hearts of women to find their purpose in life. Let us embrace the wonderful calling of God, though it is neither easy nor glamorous and there are always obstacles to overcome and seemingly more attractive ways to live. Yet God calls us to live as His ambassadors among the nations, spreading His love and making an eternal difference in the lives of those in our sphere of influence.

Prayers That Activate Fire

Lord, I ask that You will send Your fire into my life. Baptize my heart with the fire of Your love. Set Your seal of love upon my heart. Baptize me with the Holy Ghost and fire. Consume my entire being with the fire of Your presence. Lord, be a wall of fire around my life and the glory in my midst. Let me speak with tongues of fire, declaring Your Word to my generation. Let prophetic gifts be activated in my life. Give me a word of wisdom, a word of knowledge for the lost. Let me preach Your Word with fire and conviction. Let me move with gifts of healing and deliverance. Let my words be a demonstration of the Spirit and power! My faith will not be in the wisdom of men but in the power of God. Let me be a vessel of love and mercy to those who look for redemption.

I decree that every muzzle is being broken from my mouth.

I decree that I will be bold in the Lord.

I decree that I will speak against injustice.

I will be a mouthpiece for the Lord.

I will pray and preach.

I will be a voice for the voiceless.

I will prophesy to my generation.

I will preach the Word of God with signs and wonders following.

I am a living flame of love.

Notes

Introduction

1. Chris Ferguson, "Contending For Your Destiny Pt. 3," *My Soul Pants For God & God Alone* (blog), April 15, 2013, accessed July 5, 2016, https://soulpants.wordpress.com/2013/04/15/contending-for-your-destiny-pt-3/.

2. *Dictionary.com*, s.v. "indignation," accessed July 5, 2016, http://www.dictionary.com/browse/indignation.

3. *Cambridge Academic Content Dictionary*, s.v. "vigil," accessed July 5, 2016, http://dictionary.cambridge.org/us/dictionary/english/vigil.

4. Walter A. Elwell, ed., *Baker's Evangelical Dictionary of Biblical Theology* (Grand Rapids, MI: Baker, 1996), s.v. "anoint," accessed July 5, 2016, http://www.biblestudytools.com/dictionary/anoint/.

Chapter 1
Life After Loss

1. *International Standard Bible Encyclopedia*, s.v. "Anna," accessed August 9, 2016, http://www.internationalstandardbible.com/A/anna.html.

2. Rochel Holzkenner, "Asher's Beautiful Daughters," Chabad.org, accessed August 9, 2016, http://www.chabad.org/parshah/article_cdo/aid/1070734/jewish/Ashers-Beautiful-Daughters.htm.

3. Ibid.

4. *Dictionary.com*, s.v. "crisis," accessed July 5, 2016, http://www.dictionary.com/browse/crisis.

5. Warren W. Wiersbe, *The Wiersbe Bible Commentary: The Complete New Testament in One Volume* (Colorado Springs, CO: David C. Cook, 2007), 654.

6. *Blue Letter Bible*, s.v. "*eidō*," accessed September 8, 2016, https://www.blueletterbible.org/lang/lexicon/lexicon.cfm ?Strongs=G1492&t=KJV.

7. *Blue Letter Bible*, s.v. "Anna," accessed August 9, 2016, https://www.blueletterbible.org/lang/lexicon/lexicon.cfm ?Strongs=G451&t=KJV.

8. Roswell D. Hitchcock, *Hitchcock's Dictionary of Bible Names*, s.v. "Phanuel," accessed August 9, 2016, http://www .biblestudytools.com/dictionary/phanuel/.

9. Jack W. Hayford, ed., *New Spirit-Filled Life Bible: Kingdom Equipping Through the Power of the Word, New International Version* (Nashville: Thomas Nelson, 2014), 1258.

10. *Merriam-Webster Online*, s.v. "perseverance," accessed August 9, 2016, http://www.merriam-webster.com/dictionary /perseverance.

Chapter 2
Living a Life of Sacrifice

1. Rick Renner, "Idolatry and Witchcraft," *Sparkling Gems from the Greek* (blog), July 16, 2016, accessed August 9, 2016, http://www.renner.org/works-of-flesh/idolatry-and-witchcraft/.

2. Ibid.

3. Rick Renner, "Take My Yoke Upon You," *Sparkling Gems from the Greek* (blog), July 28, 2016, accessed August 9, 2016, http://www.renner.org/worry/take-my-yoke-upon-you/.

4. Rick Renner, "Present Your Bodies a Living Sacrifice," *Sparkling Gems from the Greek* (blog), November 13, 2016, accessed December 5, 2016, http://www.renner.org/christian -living/present-your-bodies-a-living-sacrifice/.

5. Michelle Haarer, *Breaking the Barriers of the Impossible* (Bloomington, IN: WestBow, 2015). Viewed at Google Books.

6. *Blue Letter Bible*, s.v. "*qavah*," accessed August 10, 2016, https://www.blueletterbible.org/lang/lexicon/lexicon.cfm ?Strongs=H6960&t=KJV.

Chapter 3
The Prophetess

1. Hayford, *New Spirit-Filled Life Bible, New International Version*, 902.

2. Nickson Banda, *Dynamics of Spiritual Warfare* (Bloomington, IN: AuthorHouse, 2010), 56.

3. John W. Ritenbaugh, *Forerunner Commentary*, "Bible Verses about Enteuxis," Bible Tools, accessed August 10, 2016, http://www.bibletools.org/index.cfm/fuseaction/Topical.show /RTD/CGG/ID/3772/Enteuxis.htm.

4. *Blue Letter Bible*, s.v. "*apokalyptō*," accessed August 10, 2016, https://www.blueletterbible.org/lang/lexicon/lexicon .cfm?Strongs=G601&t=KJV.

5. Noah Webster, *A Dictionary of English Language, Volume 2* (London: Black, Young, and Young, 1828), s.v. "revelation," 156. Viewed at Google Books.

6. *Blue Letter Bible*, s.v. "*shama'*," accessed August 10, 2016, https://www.blueletterbible.org/lang/lexicon/lexicon.cfm ?Strongs=H8085&t=KJV.

7. *Merriam-Webster Online*, s.v. "discern," accessed September 8, 2016, http://www.merriam-webster.com/dictionary /discern.

8. W. E. Vine, *Vine's Expository Dictionary of New Testament Words* (Minneapolis, MN: Bethany House, 1984), s.v. "Discern, Discerner, Discernment," accessed August 11, 2016, http://www.studylight.org/dictionaries/ved/view.cgi?n=749.

9. *Dictionary.com*, s.v. "compassion," accessed August 11, 2016, http://www.dictionary.com/browse/compassion.

10. Jack W. Hayford, ed., *New Spirit-Filled Life Bible: Kingdom Equipping Through the Power of the Word, New Living Translation* (Nashville: Thomas Nelson, 2013), 1221.

11. *Blue Letter Bible*, s.v. "*batsar*," accessed August 11, 2016, https://www.blueletterbible.org/lang/lexicon/lexicon.cfm ?Strongs=H1219&t=KJV.

Chapter 4
The Watchman/Prophet

1. *Blue Letter Bible*, s.v. "*grēgoreō*," accessed August 11, 2016, https://www.blueletterbible.org/lang/lexicon/lexicon.cfm ?Strongs=G1127&t=KJV.

2. James W. Goll, *The Lost Art of Intercession: Restoring the Power and Passion of the Watch of the Lord* (Shippensburg, PA: Destiny Image, 2007), 62.

3. *Merriam-Webster Online*, s.v. "watch," accessed August 11, 2016, http://www.merriam-webster.com/dictionary/watch.

4. J. Mark Copeland, *The Prayer Watchman* (Maitland, FL: Xulon, 2004), 32–33.

5. *Blue Letter Bible*, s.v. "*shaqad*," accessed August 11, 2016, https://www.blueletterbible.org/lang/lexicon/lexicon.cfm ?strongs=H8245.

6. "The Watchman Anointing," International House of Prayer Tallahassee Missions Base, accessed August 11, 2016, http://ihoptlh.org/wp-content/uploads/2014/12/120514_The _Watchman_Anointing.pdf.

7. *Blue Letter Bible*, s.v. "*nēphō*," accessed August 11, 2016, https://www.blueletterbible.org/lang/lexicon/lexicon.cfm ?strongs=G3525.

8. Kimberly Daniels, *Give It Back!* (Lake Mary, FL: Charisma House, 2007), 98.

9. Chuck D. Pierce, *Reordering Your Day! Understanding and Embracing the Four Prayer Watches* (Denton, TX: Glory of Zion International Ministries, 2006).

10. *Blue Letter Bible*, s.v. "*qara'*," accessed August 11, 2016, https://www.blueletterbible.org/lang/lexicon/lexicon.cfm ?Strongs=H7121&t=KJV.

11. *Blue Letter Bible*, s.v. "*'amad*," accessed August 11, 2016, https://www.blueletterbible.org/lang/lexicon/lexicon.cfm ?Strongs=H5975&t=KJV.

Chapter 5
Ministering to the Lord

1. Andrew Murray, as quoted on *Goodreads*, accessed August 11, 2016, http://www.goodreads.com/author/quotes/13326 .Andrew_Murray.

2. Mike Bickle, "Session 13 Being Taught to Pray by Jesus (Mt. 6:9–13)," International House of Prayer, accessed August 12, 2016, http://www.mikebickle.org.edgesuite.net/MikeBickle VOD/2012/20121014_Being_Taught_to_Pray_by_Jesus.pdf.

3. *Online Etymology Dictionary*, s.v. "worship," accessed August 12, 2016, http://www.etymonline.com/index.php ?term=worship.

4. *Webster's Revised Unabridged Dictionary*, s.v. "extol," accessed August 12, 2016, http://biblehub.com/topical/e/extol.htm.

5. *Baker's Evangelical Dictionary of Biblical Theology*, s.v. "greatness," accessed August 12, 2016, http://www.biblestudytools .com/dictionaries/bakers-evangelical-dictionary/greatness.html.

6. Ibid.

7. Noah Webster, *A Dictionary of the English Language, Tenth Edition* (London: George Routledge and Sons, 1866), s.v. "declare," 268.

8. *Webster's New World College Dictionary* (Cleveland, OH: Wiley, 2010), s.v. "goodness."

9. *American Dictionary of the English Language,* s.v. "righteousness," accessed August 12, 2016, http://webstersdictionary 1828.com/Dictionary/righteousness.

10. Jack W. Hayford, ed., *New Spirit-Filled Life Bible: Kingdom Equipping Through the Power of the Word, New King James Version* (Nashville: Thomas Nelson, 2002), 944.

11. *Webster's Revised Unabridged Dictionary,* s.v. "dominion," accessed August 12, 2016, http://biblehub.com/topical/d /dominion.htm.

Chapter 6
Ask, Seek, Knock

1. E. M. Bounds, as quoted on *Goodreads,* accessed August 12, 2016, https://www.goodreads.com/author/quotes/942850 .E_M_Bounds.

2. *Blue Letter Bible,* s.v. "aiteō," accessed August 12, 2016, https://www.blueletterbible.org/lang/lexicon/lexicon.cfm ?Strongs=G154&t=NKJV.

3. *Blue Letter Bible,* s.v. "hamah," accessed August 12, 2016, https://www.blueletterbible.org/lang/lexicon/lexicon.cfm ?Strongs=H1993&t=KJV.

4. *Blue Letter Bible,* s.v. "zēteō," accessed August 12, 2016, https://www.blueletterbible.org/lang/lexicon/lexicon.cfm ?Strongs=G2212&t=KJV.

5. *Thayer's Greek Lexicon,* Electronic Database. Copyright © 2002, 2003, 2006, 201 by Biblesoft, Inc. All rights reserved.

Viewed on *Bible Hub*, s.v. "krouó," accessed August 12, 2016, http://biblehub.com/greek/2925.htm.

6. *NAS Exhaustive Concordance of the Bible with Hebrew-Aramaic and Greek Dictionaries.* Copyright © 1981, 1998 by The Lockman Foundation. All rights reserved. Viewed on *Bible Hub*, s.v. "paga," accessed August 12, 2016, http://biblehub.com/hebrew/6293.htm.

7. *Merriam-Webster Online*, s.v. "travail," accessed August 12, 2016, http://www.merriam-webster.com/dictionary/travail.

Chapter 7
Identification Intercession

1. Andrew Murray, *The Ministry of Intercession*, 3rd ed. (London: James Nisbet & Co. Limited, 1898), 53.

2. "World-Wide Population," The Traveling Team, accessed August 15, 2016, http://www.thetravelingteam.org/stats/.

3. *Merriam-Webster Online*, s.v. "restore," accessed August 15, 2016, http://www.merriam-webster.com/dictionary/restore.

4. James Robison, "The Holy Spirit and Restoration," in *New Spirit-Filled Life Bible: Kingdom Equipping Through the Power of the Word, New King James Version*, ed. Jack W. Hayford (Nashville: Thomas Nelson, 2002), 1859.

5. *Dictionary.com*, s.v. "indifference," accessed August 15, 2016, http://www.dictionary.com/browse/indifference.

6. *Merriam-Webster Online*, s.v. "hardened," accessed August 15, 2016, http://www.merriam-webster.com/dictionary/hardened; *Dictionary.com*, s.v. "hardened," accessed August 15, 2016, http://www.dictionary.com/browse/hardened?s=t; Martin H. Manser, *Dictionary of Bible Themes*, s.v. "6178 Hardness of Heart," 2009, accessed August 15, 2016, http://biblehub.com/topical/dbt/6178.htm.

7. *Dictionary of Bible Themes*, s.v. "6178 Hardness of Heart," accessed August 15, 2016, http://biblehub.com/topical/dbt /6178.htm.

Chapter 8
Developing the Spirit of Grace and Supplication

1. Andrew Murray, *With Christ in the School of Prayer* (New York: Fleming H. Revell Company, 1885), ix.

2. *Blue Letter Bible*, s.v. "'Iy-kabowd," accessed August 15, 2016, https://www.blueletterbible.org/lang/lexicon/lexicon .cfm?Strongs=H350&t=KJV.

3. *Blue Letter Bible*, s.v. "Ya`aqob," accessed August 15, 2016, https://www.blueletterbible.org/lang/lexicon/lexicon.cfm ?Strongs=H3290&t=KJV.

4. C. J. Ellicott, *Ellicott's Commentary for English Readers*, s.v. "Genesis 32:28," accessed August 15, 2016, http://biblehub.com /commentaries/genesis/32-28.htm.

5. Abarim Publications, "Anna Meaning," accessed August 15, 2016, http://www.abarim-publications.com/Meaning/Anna .html#.V7H4UpgrIdV.

6. R. Laird Harris, Gleason L. Archer, and Bruce K. Waltke, *The Theological Wordbook of the Old Testament* (Chicago: Moody, 1908), 302.

7. Abarim, "Anna Meaning."

8. *Merriam-Webster Online*, s.v. "beseech," accessed August 15, 2016, http://www.merriam-webster.com/dictionary/beseech.

9. David M. Edwards, *Worship 365: The Power of a Worshiping Life* (Nashville, TN: B&H Publishing Group, 2006), 41.

10. Dr. Moses Anyanwu, *Divine Messages and Inspirations* (n.p.: Xlibris, 2012). Viewed at Google Books.

11. *Blue Letter Bible*, s.v. *"synantilambanomai,"* accessed August 15, 2016, https://www.blueletterbible.org/lang/lexicon /lexicon.cfm?Strongs=G4878&t=KJV.

12. *Blue Letter Bible*, s.v. *"astheneia,"* accessed August 15, 2016, https://www.blueletterbible.org/lang/lexicon/lexicon.cfm ?Strongs=G769&t=KJV.

13. *Blue Letter Bible*, s.v. *"dei,"* accessed August 15, 2016, https://www.blueletterbible.org/lang/lexicon/lexicon.cfm ?Strongs=G1163&t=KJV.

14. Rick Renner, "The Supernatural Intercessory Ministry of the Holy Spirit," *Sparkling Gems from the Greek* (blog), March 29, 2016, accessed August 15, 2016, http://www.renner.org /holy-spirit/the-supernatural-intercessory-ministry-of-the-holy -spirit/.

15. *Blue Letter Bible*, s.v. *"stenagmos,"* accessed August 15, 2016, https://www.blueletterbible.org/lang/lexicon/lexicon .cfm?Strongs=G4726&t=KJV.

16. *Blue Letter Bible*, s.v. *"alalētos,"* accessed August 15, 2016, https://www.blueletterbible.org/lang/lexicon/lexicon.cfm ?Strongs=G215&t=KJV.

17. *Blue Letter Bible*, s.v. *"eraunaō,"* accessed August 15, 2016, https://www.blueletterbible.org/lang/lexicon/lexicon.cfm ?Strongs=G2045&t=KJV.

18. *Blue Letter Bible*, s.v. *"phronēma,"* accessed August 15, 2016, https://www.blueletterbible.org/lang/lexicon/lexicon .cfm?Strongs=G5427&t=KJV.

Chapter 9
The Worshipping Warrior

1. *Blue Letter Bible*, s.v. *"palē,"* accessed August 15, 2016, https://www.blueletterbible.org/lang/lexicon/lexicon.cfm ?Strongs=G3823&t=KJV.

2. *Merriam-Webster Online*, s.v. "resist," accessed August 15, 2016, http://www.merriam-webster.com/dictionary/resist.

3. Hayford, *New Spirit-Filled Life Bible, New King James*, 1654.

4. John F. MacArthur, *The MacArthur New Testament Commentary* (Chicago: Moody, 2011), s.v. "Ephesians 6:14."

5. *Blue Letter Bible*, s.v. "*alētheia*," accessed August 15, 2016, https://www.blueletterbible.org/lang/lexicon/lexicon.cfm?Strongs=G225&t=KJV.

Chapter 10
God's Minister of Fire

1. Leland Ryken, James C. Wilhoit, and Tremper Longman III, eds., *Dictionary of Biblical Imagery*, s.v. "Seal" (Downers Grove, IL: InterVarsity, 1998), 766.

2. Mike Bickle, "The Bridal Seal of Mature Love," International House of Prayer, accessed August 16, 2016, http://www.mikebickle.org.edgesuite.net/MikeBickleVOD/2007/20070902_The_Bridal_Seal_of_Mature_Love_SOS23.pdf.

3. *Blue Letter Bible*, s.v. "*parrēsia*," accessed August 16, 2016, https://www.blueletterbible.org/lang/lexicon/lexicon.cfm?Strongs=G3954&t=KJV.

CONNECT WITH US!

CHARISMA HOUSE

(Spiritual Growth)

f Facebook.com/CharismaHouse

@CharismaHouse

Instagram.com/CharismaHouse

SILOAM

(Health)

Pinterest.com/CharismaHouse

MEV MODERN ENGLISH VERSION

(Bible)
www.mevbible.com